Teachers and Human Rights Education

Teachers and Human Rights Education

Audrey Osler and Hugh Starkey

A Trentham Book

Institute of Education Press, London

Institute of Education Press
20 Bedford Way
London
WC1H 0AL

First published 2010

British Library Cataloguing-in-Publication Data
A catalogue record for this book is available from the
British Library

ISBN: 978 1 85856 384 8

Printed by CPI Group (UK) Ltd, Croydon, CR0 4YY

Contents

Part 3: Human rights and democracy in schools

Teachers and Human Rights Education is dedicated to the memory
of

Steve Sinnott

1951-2008

General Secretary of the National Union of Teachers

A powerful advocate of human rights education and children's rights
in education both in Britain and internationally. Steve put human
rights principles into action in daily life through his loyal
support of friends and colleagues.

Acknowledgements

We wish to acknowledge the contributions of our students and of our friends and colleagues across the globe, in the academy, in NGOs, and in international organisations, who have influenced our thinking and practice in human rights education over more than two decades.

We thank, in particular, our editor Dr Gillian Klein, who has shown tremendous patience and support in the process of realising this project.

We are grateful to the National Union of Teachers (NUT) for permission to use the cover picture and to Samidha Garg and Hellen Njie for their kind help in facilitating this. It is from a child in India who took part in an education campaign. Children wrote letters and made drawings about their hopes and dreams for their futures. The NUT coordinated the efforts of teachers and children across the Commonwealth into a Bigbook Campaign. This drawing was included in a Bigbook of children's work presented to Gordon Brown MP, at the Commonwealth Finance Ministers' meeting in London, in 2002.

Chapter one includes a narrative inspired by the acclaimed South African film, *Yesterday*, which won an award at the Venice Film Festival in 2004. *Yesterday* was produced by Anant Singh and directed by Darrell James Roodt. The cast include Leleti Khumalo, Lihle Mvelase, Kenneth Kambule, and Harriet Lehabe. We appreciate their inspiration and warmly thank Darrell James Roodt for permission to draw on his work.

Figure 4.5 draws on *Voices from the Holocaust education* materials © British Library. We thank the British Library for permission to use these.

Chapter nine contains material adapted from: Osler, A. (2009) Human rights education and education for democratic citizenship: competing or complimentary agendas? In: C. Mahler, A. Mihr and R. Toivanen (eds.)*The United Nations Decade for Human Rights Education and the inclusion of national minorities.* Frankfurt: Peter Lang, 55-65.

Osler, A. (2010) Citizenship and the nation-state: affinity, identity and belonging, in: A. Reid, J. Gill and A. Sears (eds.) *Globalization, the Nation-State and the Citizen: Dilemmas and Directions for Civics and Citizenship Education.* Routledge: New York, 216-222.

Acronyms and abbreviations

ADFM	Association Démocratique des Femmes du Maroc
AI	Amnesty International
ANC	African National Congress
CAT	Convention against Torture and Other Cruel, Inhuman or Degrading Treatment or Punishment 1984
CCSE	Centre for Citizenship Studies in Education
CEDAW	Convention on the Elimination of all Forms of Discrimination Against Women 1979
CRC	Convention on the Rights of the Child 1989
CRPD	Convention on the Rights of Persons with Disabilities 2006
CWRIC	Commission on Wartime Relocation and Internment of Civilians
DfES	Department for Education and Skills
ECHR	European Convention on Human Rights and Fundamental Freedoms
EDC	Education for Democratic Citizenship
EIHRN	Education in Human Rights Network
EIP	Association Mondiale Ecole Instrument de Paix (School as an instrument of peace)
ESRC	Economic and Social Research Council
FCO	Foreign and Commonwealth Office
FRA	European Union Agency for Fundamental Rights
GCE	Global Campaign for Education
HRE	Human Rights Education
HREA	Human Rights Education Associates
ICERD	International Convention on the Elimination of All Forms of Racial Discrimination 1965
ICCPR	International Covenant on Civil and Political Rights 1966

ICESCR	International Covenant on Economic, Social and Cultural Rights1966
ICPD	International Conference on Population and Development, Cairo, 1994
ICPPED	International Convention for the Protection of All Persons from Enforced Disappearance 2006
ICRMW	International Convention on the Protection of the Rights of All Migrant Workers and Members of Their Families 1990
ILO	International Labour Organisation
IMF	International Monetary Fund
MDG	Millennium Development Goal
MPH	Make Poverty History
NEA	National Education Association
NUT	National Union of Teachers
NGO	Non-Governmental Organisation
OECD	Organisation for Economic Co-operation and Development
OHCHR	United Nations Office of the High Commissioner for Human Rights
QCA	Qualifications and Curriculum Authority
SBS	Southall Black Sisters
UDHR	Universal Declaration of Human Rights 1948
UK	United Kingdom of Great Britain and Northern Ireland
UN	United Nations
UNO	United Nations Organisation
UNDP	United Nations Development Programme
UNESCO	United Nations Education, Scientific and Cultural Organisation
UNICPD	International Conference on Population and Development
UNICEF	United Nations Children's Fund
US	United States of America
USSR	Union of Soviet Socialist Republics
WHO	World Health Organisation
WPHRE	World Programme for Human Rights Education
YCC	Youth Citizenship Commission

Foreword

I was delighted when I heard that Audrey Osler and Hugh Starkey were working on a new volume entitled *Teachers and Human Rights Education*, taking forward many of the themes from their 1996 collaboration, *Teacher Education and Human Rights*.

That volume emerged during an upbeat period for the human rights project at a time when there was an increasing global commitment to human rights education. The Council of Europe Recommendation on Human Rights Education 1985, the Convention on the Rights of the Child 1989, and the Vienna Declaration 1993 were all standard-setting texts helpful to the human rights-friendly teacher. This embrace of rights as a tool for empowerment, emancipation and citizenship reflected and stimulated the geopolitical mood of the time: the end of the Cold War; the end of Apartheid; and peace in Northern Ireland. There was a recommitment to the indivisibility of all rights, reflected not least with the emergence of human rights-based approaches to global development. So it was with optimism that we headed into the UN Decade for Human Rights Education (1995-2004).

There was urgency in this work, for clearly not everything was well with the world. Xenophobia was rising across Europe; horrific conflicts continued in Sierra Leone, the Democratic Republic of the Congo and elsewhere; there was rising inequality in the former USSR and Asia as the seeds of globalisation were sown; and authoritarianism and dictatorship persisted in Latin America.

The compelling message that Audrey and Hugh had for educators and governments alike was that teachers must be given the knowledge, understanding and skills to teach in, for and through human rights. They provided the evidence base, and outlined the legally binding frameworks that showed how teacher education is intrinsic to human rights. They showed us how human rights-friendly teachers can become the catalysts for a new generation of empowered and active citizens. By teaching children in an environment where they experience equality, fairness, dignity, and inclusion, we contribute to a more just world.

As a school principal in Ireland at the time I became extremely interested in the work that Audrey and Hugh were doing, and was subsequently fortunate enough to study for a PhD with Audrey with an action research study on human rights education in my own school. I went on to work in this area with Amnesty International and was involved in the establishment of the first teacher training centre dedicated to human rights education at the Dublin City University's St Patrick's College of Education.

Since 1996, Audrey and Hugh have continued their research, practice, teaching and writing with a passion and commitment that has inspired students and educators across the globe. They are two of the most influential scholars and practitioners of human rights education worldwide.

In the course of their academic work on human rights education they have engaged with ministries of education, teacher training colleges, inter-governmental organisations and civil society on all continents for over twenty years. Their wide range of publications have consistently pushed for and provided evidence to prove that educating people about their rights is good for democracy, for citizenship and for society.

They were among the first to frame the right to know your rights, and the importance of rights as a methodology. Their work over the years successfully integrates three essential components that together underpin human rights education in the formal school system:

1) An in-depth knowledge and interpretation of international human rights law and normative legal frameworks relating to human rights education, together with national laws and standards on education. This rootedness in the binding duties on nation-states, in the Convention on the Rights of the Child for example, has given legitimacy to their call for teachers to be tooled for human rights education.

2) By studying curriculum, school structure, management, training and the systems of education they have collected the research and case studies from schools and classrooms that provide the evidence and examples to show that rights-friendly teachers are changing lives.

3) Most importantly, they reflect the stories and testimonies of people's experiences in the school system. The stories come from students experiencing discrimination, insecurity, and exclusion because the education system and the people that make it work are so often blind

to human rights. The views of their teachers and principals underscore the need for teachers to be exposed to human rights education methodologies in pre-service and in-service training.

Together this human story of institutional failure, the evidence of success in human rights-friendly schools, and the legally binding obligations to teach children their rights, illustrate the vital connections between teachers and human rights education.

This new volume is timely and highly significant, not least because the mood of optimism from the 1990s has been dulled. Since then we have seen the introduction of discriminatory laws, increasing polarisation, and the erosion of human rights in the name of security. The climate of anxiety and fear sown by the combined horrors of terrorism and draconian counter-terror responses has been exploited to undermine rights. This row-back on liberties is creeping into formal education systems too.

The World Decade on Human Rights Education and the subsequent World Programme for Human Rights Education which has been running since 2005 with a focus on the school system have had little political backing at national level, and resulted in few qualified examples of increased commitment to human rights education. No surprise perhaps that nation-states would not want to empower their citizens to play an active participatory role in society with the full knowledge and understanding of their rights. So this duality where nation-states gladly sign up to tokenistic strategies to promote rights while blocking participation rights and real empowerment through human rights education needs to be challenged. And this book is one more important step on that road, emphasising the fundamental position teachers hold regarding human rights education.

I was honoured to be invited to pen the preface to this book, for I cannot think of a more meaningful, effective and impactful way to bring dignity and justice to our world than to teach all teachers how to teach in human rights.

Dr Colm Ó Cuanacháin
Senior Director of Campaigns
Amnesty International

Part 1
Human rights: an agenda for action

1

Three narratives

When the Universal Declaration of Human Rights (UDHR) was proclaimed in 1948, it was, in the words of the preamble, in 'recognition of the inherent dignity and of the equal and inalienable rights of all members of the human family [which] is the foundation of freedom, justice and peace in the world'. The Universal Declaration was conceived and drafted in the period immediately following World War II, a period in which there were gross abuses of human rights and when civilian populations across the world were denied dignity, equality, and security.

This first chapter of *Teachers and Human Rights Education* presents three narratives. One narrative is set in North America, the second in South East Asia, and the third in Southern Africa. Each of the narratives is designed to raise key human rights issues and problems. The intention in the first two narratives is to illustrate aspects of the historical context in which present day human rights were introduced and developed. The narratives also emphasise that the human rights project is ongoing and that it remains important, regardless of geographical or cultural context. In the words of the UDHR, human rights belong equally to 'all members of the human family'. The ultimate aim is the realisation of justice and peace.

Yet the narratives highlight everyday injustices and violence which continue at the beginning of the twenty-first century, when the third narrative is set. The realisation of human rights, justice and peace, together with proper recognition of the equal dignity of all, demand on-going commitment and action from current generations, from both governments and civil society, including children and young people.

Two of the narratives begin in December 1941 and are set in wartime. Both are a reflection of the impact of war on the lives of civilians, and on the lives of young people in particular. The first narrative begins on the west coast of the United States, following the attack on Pearl Harbour on 7 December 1941. The narrator, Yoriko, is a fictional character, but her account reflects the experiences of thousands of real American citizens who were incarcerated by their own government during World War II. They were told their enforced placement in camps was for their own security. At the time, most of their fellow Americans accepted unquestioningly the actions of the authorities.

Yoriko's story draws on a range of primary sources from the 1940s and on recorded recollections from later decades. In 1980, President Jimmy Carter and the US Congress established the Commission on Wartime Relocation and Internment of Civilians (CWRIC) in response to pressure from Japanese-American activists who were seeking an official apology and redress for what they and their families had suffered at the hands of the government.

The CWRIC was charged to collect evidence to determine whether any wrongs had been done to these civilians during World War II. Some 750 witnesses testified to the 1981 congressional hearings of the CWRIC (CWRIC, [1983] 1996). Yoriko's fictional narrative draws on a range of genuine historical primary sources, notably on letters, testimonies to the Commission and other materials assembled and published by Joanne Oppenheim (2006).

The second narrative runs parallel in time to the first and is set in Singapore. The second narrator, Esmé, describes her experiences and those of her family, living under the rule of the occupying Japanese Imperial Army. Her story begins just one day after that of Yoriko, on 8 December 1941, when the Japanese forces attacked the Malay peninsula. This narrative is a genuine first-hand account, part of a life history told to and recorded by Audrey, more than 60 years after the events took place. Singapore was at that time part of the British Empire and its people were British subjects. As the invading army approached, the British authorities evacuated (white) British civilians and military personnel. Esmé and her family were left to their fate, along with other Singapore inhabitants of Malay, Chinese, Indian, and mixed descent.

The episode highlights the fragility and value of the British classification as applied to colonial peoples: in the crisis of war and invasion colonial (non-white) civilians lost their protection while (predominantly white) civilians from the UK assumed full entitlement to on-going protection.

Both Yoriko's story and that of Esmé, although they recall experiences from the first half of the twentieth century, address a range of rights and freedoms which are routinely denied in times of war. Esmé's narrative also reflects the experiences of children in times of conflict and armed occupation which continue today, including disruption to education and family life, malnutrition, and threats to physical and psychological health and well-being.

Both stories have resonance at the beginning of the twenty-first century, when civilian populations continue to experience the impact of occupation, war and conflict and where in a number of countries, including Britain, there is continuing debate about restrictions to rights and freedoms imposed by government, in the name of security and in response to the so-called war on terror. Both narratives also reveal the strength and resilience of human beings, young and old, and the role of human agency, particularly solidarity, resistance and friendship. In this respect the first two narratives share features with the third.

The third narrator is an unnamed teacher, living in South Africa in the early years of the twenty-first century. The teacher is a fictional character, but the events described are all too common. The narrative is inspired by the award winning film *Yesterday*, produced by Anant Singh and directed by Darrell James Roodt. The authors of this book first heard about the film from students at Zola High School, in Khayelitsha Township, Cape Town. They told us: 'You must see this film. It is about our lives.' In fact, the film is not about the urban experiences of these young people, since it is set in rural KwaZulu Natal. The film is however about the experiences of millions of South Africans, since it tells of the tragic impact of HIV AIDS on the lives of a family and a community. The film is a reminder of the on-going importance of human rights and human rights education.

In the teacher's narrative we hear about human rights issues which are in some ways different from, yet in others similar to, those faced by the first two narrators. Health remains a key human rights issue across the globe, in both developed and developing countries. The problem of HIV AIDS is also faced by people across the globe, although in some countries, including South Africa, its impact has been devastating, leading not only to individual suffering and poverty, but threatening the economic stability and development of communities, the nation and region. In order to address effectively the question of HIV AIDS and a wide range of other issues including food security, environmental questions, and access to quality education, governments and civil society must necessarily cooperate both within and across national borders, drawing also on the resources and influence of inter-governmental organisations.

The need for human solidarity is examined in subsequent chapters. The key point here is that these stories and others like them need to be told and re-told. Even if such narratives at first seem remote from our experiences, the impact of war, conflict, and threats to human rights impact directly or indirectly on the wider global community. The forces of globalisation mean that problems in one region affect others elsewhere, whether they live in relatively prosperous or developing nations, through the impact of refugees, economic migrants, trade, environmental damage and shortages of scarce resources. Such narratives are, as the young people in Khayelitsha, Cape Town recognised, not just about strangers but also about our lives.

Yoriko's story
San Francisco, USA

My name is Yoriko Karasawa. My family call me Yori but I've always been known as Kathy to my friends. I was born in San Diego. My mother was also born in California and my father came to the United States as a child with his parents. On December 7, 1941, the Japanese Imperial forces attacked the American naval base in Pearl Harbor. I was just fourteen. As soon as we heard the news, we were filled with fear.

That night two men came to our house and arrested my father. He was a business-man and was seen as a leader in the local Japanese-American community. He left without a word of protest. In the eyes of the authorities, he posed some kind of threat to the United States. We did not see him again for nearly three years. He had done nothing illegal and he was never charged with any crime. That day changed the lives of our family and all other Japanese-American families living in California and along the West Coast.

The following day at school, we listened to President Roosevelt making his speech about war. There were five or six Japanese-American kids in our class. Although our class was very mixed, we shared a school bus with another school. Some children, and even the bus driver, made us feel uncomfortable. Some shops had signs in the windows saying: 'No Japs'. From that point on I dreaded going to school.

Early in the New Year the whole of the West Coast was declared a war zone and we began to hear reports that we would be moved inland or to detention centers. My teacher told me my family would be OK, since me, my mother and my bother and sisters were all U.S. citizens and would be protected by the Constitution. A few days later we received our papers to evacuate. One day we were living as citizens in a democracy, the next we were being treated as enemies.

We had very little time to prepare. We weren't able to take much with us. We arranged to store some of our most precious things with neighbors and some at the Buddhist temple. The rest we put in a yard sale, although people offered my mother a pittance, knowing we had no choice but to sell. I gave my best doll and the few books I had to one of my school friends. I had long grown out of the doll, but it was difficult all the same. On April 7, 1942, just four months after Pearl Harbor, we went to the railway station and waited to board the train. We had no real idea where they were sending us, just rumors.

After a long journey by train and then bus, we arrived at our destination, Santa Anita camp. It was described as an assembly center but there were watchtowers around the outside, with searchlights, and we were guarded by armed solders and military police. We were housed in a former stable and before we could move in we had to scrub it clean. We never got rid of the smell of the horses. There was no school and the little kids had a great time, playing all day. At first, we relished the freedom we had to wander about the camp and play sports, but it wasn't long before we missed the routine of school. Although my mother put on a brave face, it was clear that many of the adults were very distressed. We remained there until August. Eventually, they told us we would be transferred to Arizona.

Some days later, and a twenty hour ride by train and then bus, we found ourselves in our new home, Poston; rows upon rows of tar-papered wooden barracks, in the middle of a dry, dusty desert. Everyone over seventeen had to be fingerprinted on arrival. Our family had their own room, but smaller families had to share. Each block shared a latrine. The nearest town was sixteen miles away. The week we arrived the temperature was more than 120 degrees Fahrenheit. It felt like an oven, with the hot air hitting you in the face. At that time I had a constant heat rash. Poston was built on Indian land, and there were 18,000 Japanese-Americans living in three separate camps. We felt completely cut off from our old lives in San Diego and from the rest of the world. It was hard to imagine that our new home was even on the map!

In the fall, after six months enforced vacation, we looked forward to returning to school and meeting our new teachers. They must have had some difficulty recruiting enough teachers, because for the first couple of weeks there were some changes. To begin with there were no desks, chairs, books, or chalkboards. It was suddenly very strange to find ourselves in classes where we were all Japanese. We knew that the Caucasian teachers were paid eight or nine times the wages of their Japanese-American colleagues and I think we tended to see the Caucasian teachers in a different light. In San Diego our classes had been much more mixed. I remember celebrating the first Thanksgiving holiday in Poston. People decorated the large communal dining room with wild flowers.

In January 1943, we heard that that there had been a fire at the Buddhist temple in San Diego, and we feared we had lost most of our possessions. Then in February the Army arrived and began to recruit young men into a special Japanese-American combat unit. Many volunteered, anxious to prove their loyalty to the United States.

In the summer, we girls found very little had changed, but some of the boys were allowed to leave the camp for a few weeks, to help bring in the harvest. My brother went to Idaho, because there was a labor shortage. But he had a very bad experience. There were signs around town saying 'No Japs allowed'. And people harassed them, even though they were doing their bit for the war effort.

Towards the end of 1943 people were allowed to leave the camp, but my mother was waiting for my father to be released. We had the option of joining him in the camp in Texas where he had been sent, but she was concerned that if we went there we children would have little schooling and might not be free to leave until the war was over.

From Spring 1944, the military draft was applied to Japanese-Americans and it was then that my older brother joined the army. In June 1944, I was in the first group of students to graduate from the new Parker Valley High School in Poston. We were very lucky since our principal managed to get the high school accredited, meaning that there was still a chance we could go to college. For many teenagers sent to camps, this was an option taken from them. In November 1944 my father was released. After a long discussion, my parents decided to return to San Diego. My sisters and I were very excited to be going home, but my parents were much more worried as to what we would find.

Esmé's story
Hemel Hempstead, UK

My name is Esmé and I was born in Miri, in Sarawak, in 1927. My parents had migrated from Madras in India, and I spent some of the first years of my life there. When I was about seven years old we moved to Singapore, where my father found work.

The Japanese army arrived in Malaya on 8 December 1941. They marched and rode bicycles through the Malay Peninsula, occupying the whole country. We were on our school break. I was nearly fifteen and I had just finished my O levels.

Singapore held out for several weeks. My father was in the civil defence. There were Australians and New Zealanders in Singapore helping us. The Japanese were dropping bombs on us – we hid in the monsoon drains. The British were evacuated to India. On February 15 Singapore surrendered. The Japanese remained for three and a half years. We never went back to school again.

We all had to register in so-called national groups: Chinese, Indians, Malays and Eurasians. The Japanese didn't trust the Chinese and each hated the other. They took some of the young Chinese men – and some older men – and they shot them. It was said at the time that the Indians did not pose a problem to the Japanese since all they were thinking of was Independence. Many people lost their lives. On one occasion we heard how men had been beheaded and the heads displayed in town. My elder brother Dudley went to see for himself.

The occupying forces interned a lot of people. Any British that remained were put in Outram Road prison in Changi. At first everything was chaotic. They took our home, which was in town, and commandeered it for their own use. We had nowhere to go. My father had a friend in some sort of local government and he created a job for him. We moved into some unfinished bungalows in Yiochukang, on Serangoon Road. We had no running water and had to use a well.

To begin with, once things settled down, town was fine but things got worse. The Japanese soldiers did not really bother us, but my cousin was taken away. They said she was raped. She was taken to live with this Japanese man. She had a baby, but she lost it. She got tuberculosis.

I remember one night that some Chinese men came to our house. They wanted help from my father to enable some British men- some runaways- to escape. I'm not sure if he did this on more than one occasion. But we children did not really know what was going on- it was dangerous and it was important that we knew very little.

We were all undernourished. My father got beriberi. My mother and I both had malaria, because they weren't able to keep the place clean. In Yiochukang we had a garden and we grew some vegetables, sweet potatoes and tapioca, because the rations for a month only lasted for two weeks. The bread was like rubber. By the end of the war my mother had lost a lot of weight and we just had two dresses between us, which we shared.

A Japanese officer who lived on his own nearby would sometimes come and sit with my father in the evening and talk. My younger brother Ralph had to work for the telephone company and I found a job. The trolley buses were very unreliable and the transport system was breaking down. This officer, Kakamoto, got us transport into town to work. I would carry vegetables with me into town to share with family and friends. Sometimes I had to walk the four miles or so back home after work, and I was sick for much of this time with malaria.

In our lunch break we were offered Japanese lessons. In return we received a ration of rice. So this was very attractive. We learnt some Japanese children's songs. We were asked to go the military camp and sing them. My father was not at all happy about this but there was little we could do, once we had agreed. It worked out all right, but I never went again.

After a short while we were forced to move out from our place in Yiochukang. The Japanese took the bungalow. We lost our garden and the food. But when my father was admitted to hospital with beriberi, Kakamoto came and visited him and placed some money under his pillow.

One of our other neighbours, a Malaya-born Chinese woman (a nonya) was living with her partner, her son and her servant. Her partner volunteered to work on the railway; what became known as the Siam Death Railway. When the Japanese took the bungalow she invited us, my mother, father, and younger brother to stay in one room. This woman had only two bedrooms and a kitchen and toilet.

You weren't supposed to listen to the radio broadcasts, but some people did. We knew something about the atomic bomb when it was dropped on Hiroshima in August 1945. We knew the Japanese were losing the war. When the bomb was dropped, Kakamoto broke down and cried.

A teacher's story
Durban, South Africa

My story begins in the summer time, in 2002, in the eastern part of KwaZulu Natal province, South Africa. I was walking with my friend. We are teachers and, although the school year was about to start, we had not found work. We were travelling from village to village, looking for a school that needed teachers. We had been travelling for a long time. That morning we set out at dawn, and although it was still quite early, the sun was already hot.

We came upon a young woman and her small daughter at a crossroads. We greeted her and explained we were looking for work. She told us her name was Leleti. She had a beautiful smile. It is Leleti's story, and that of her little girl, that I want to tell you.

Leleti told us there was a school in her village but she didn't know whether they needed any teachers. She explained it was a two hour walk. She was on her way to the clinic. She had a stubborn cough and she wanted to get it checked.

That day turned out to be a good day for me in more ways than I first realised. I was fortunate enough to find work in Leleti's village, and shortly afterwards I started at the school. The day I arrived, Leleti came to welcome me. She had met my friend on her way back from the clinic and heard of my good fortune. Good news, as well as bad, travels fast. Leleti took me to the water pump and introduced me to the village women. She made me feel so welcome. It seems that my good fortune doubled, for I made a good friend.

I was concerned about Leleti. Her cough was no better, but she hadn't managed to see a doctor. The queues at the clinic are long. Two times she returned home without help. Then she collapsed outside her house. It was her small daughter, Grace, who had found her. Imagine! It must have been quite a shock for the child to find her mother lying on the ground. I think Leleti was also quite frightened. She went to see the Sangoma, the village traditional healer.

The following week, I insisted Leleti travel by taxi to the clinic. I couldn't bear to think what would happen if she collapsed by the side of the road. I looked after the child. Leleti came back her cheerful self. She couldn't get over the idea that the young blond doctor could speak Zulu! She wanted to pay for the taxi fare, but I pointed out that she had already paid me more than enough in kindness. I told my new friend how I am looking forward to teaching the child when she starts school.

A week or so later, Leleti told me she needed to visit her husband, Peter. She says he's a good man. He works as a migrant worker in one of the Johannesburg gold mines. She left the child with me. It's a long, long journey. I've never been there myself so I couldn't give her much help. I'm not sure what passed between them, but she came back quite distressed, and her face was badly bruised.

Six months or so later, during the winter, Leleti's husband came back home. I thought, at least she will now have someone to help her on the land. Leleti did not have a strong constitution. But I did not see him leave the house, and very soon the village women were gossiping, asking if he is sick.

The village women say Leleti's husband has AIDS. Leleti told me that a woman in a neighbouring village was stoned to death for having the virus. It was then she told me the news. Her husband was very sick, much too sick to work, and they sent him home from the mine. But this was not the worst. Leleti also has the virus. Yet she is a strong willed woman. She told me: 'Until my child goes to school, I will not die. I never had the chance to go to school. I can't read or write. I want a better future for my child'.

Leleti tried to get a bed for her husband at the hospital, but the waiting list was long. I tried to talk to the women and to explain Peter is not a risk to their health or that of their families. But they are superstitious and they don't believe me. Some of them threatened the family. So Leleti built a shack out in the fields, way outside the village, and she took her husband and child up there, so he could die in peace and with a degree of dignity.

About a year after I arrived in the village, during the summer, Leleti became very sick. She lost a great deal of weight and her face was covered in sores. But this time she was determined no one would drive her out. I told her: 'When the time comes I will care for your daughter as if she is my own.'

Leleti began sewing her daughter a dress. The evening before the new school year began, Leleti presented Grace with her new school uniform. On the first day she proudly took Grace to school, smiling and waiting until the child was safely inside the classroom.

Grace is now ten years old and has been enrolled in school for three years. I have left the village and I am teaching in Durban. I have kept my promise to Leleti and am bringing her up as if she were my own child. She has happy memories of her mother and I encourage her to talk about her. When I met Leleti on the road that day, I could never have imagined how that meeting would lead to me adopting a child!

Grace spent two years in the village school, and then she moved with me to the city. Her mother wanted her to have the education she herself never had, but it's a struggle ensuring that a child flourishes in a small village like that, as an AIDS orphan. We insisted the children treat each other with respect, but it is a much bigger task educating the whole community.

Discussion

United States citizens who spoke out against the incarceration of Japanese-Americans in 1942 risked the consequences of being judged unpatriotic at a time of war. The incarceration was able to happen due to the indifference of millions of their fellow citizens, and the hostility of others. Although in the 1940s racism was a fact of everyday life for many Americans, there was nevertheless a principle of racial equality. The principle was not rooted in law; quite the reverse, and the principle itself was abandoned in a moment of crisis. As Eleanor Roosevelt noted:

> They [Japanese-Americans] were marked out as different from other races and they were not treated on an equal basis. This happened because in one part of our country they were feared as competitors, and the rest of our country knew about them so little and cared so little about them that they did not even think about the principle that we in this country believe in – that of equal rights for all human beings. (quoted in Oppenheim, 2006:21)

Ironically, this neglect of the principle of the equal rights of all human beings, and the mass incarceration of citizens on the sole basis of race, was occurring as the nation entered a war against fascism and against Germany, which was engaging in the mass killing of members of its own citizenry, those who were Jewish and other groups who were labelled as inferior.

This episode in US history is a reminder to those who assert that tolerance is a virtue, that tolerance, although important, is usually an inadequate response, particularly if it implies neutrality or indifference. Tolerance means very little if minorities do not enjoy equal protection under the law and if tolerance is not underpinned by a sound understanding of human rights. We generally have no need to tolerate those we like or whom we recognise as our equals. Tolerance towards a group generally implies dislike or disapproval and often implies their assumed inferiority.

Tolerance towards minorities, as expressed in Europe today, for example, is often an 'ignorant tolerance' (Beck, 1998:133) which is fragile in time of crisis. So, for example, since 2001 and more particularly since the London bombings of 2005, sections of the British popular press have reflected and strengthened a pre-existing current of Islamophobia, which was previously held in check by a contrary tendency or societal belief that tolerance is an important British characteristic (Osler, 2009a).

Similarly, in Germany at the beginning of the twenty-first century, there are tensions and inconsistencies between ambitions of multicultural tolerance and cosmopolitanism on the one hand, and race-based ideologies of blood and belonging, which place the Turkish minority as 'other'. Mandel (2008) draws comparisons between the ways in which Germany's current Turkish population of two million are positioned in relation to 'ethnic Germans' and the past positioning of Germany's Jewish population. The limits of toleration in Europe today can be measured in response to the following questions: who is considered a real German, a real Dane, or a real Englishman or woman?

War and poverty both bring into sharp focus a number of human rights issues. The narratives raise issues not just about equality and racial discrimination, but also a range of other issues, including those relating to arbitrary arrest and access to a hearing; inhumane treatment; equal pay for equal work; health; food; housing; medical care; and education.

Universal good quality and free primary education is one of the eight millennium development goals (MDGs). Yet many children who enrol in school today, particularly girls, are unable to finish their schooling or even successfully complete their primary education. This is an issue (one of many in our globalised world) which cannot be resolved at national levels. It requires co-operation between nations and cooperation between citizens of those nations, building on a sense of common identity and solidarity as human beings. It requires us to develop a cosmopolitan imagination.

Before World War II, most legal scholars would probably have agreed that there was little or nothing in international law to impede any sovereign power from gross mistreatment of its own citizens. The UDHR represented a set of principles against which nation-states might be subjected to moral pressure. Since 1948 these principles have gained strength since many have been codified in other international agreements and in national constitutions.

Access to effective justice is still not available to many people in the most disadvantaged circumstances. Nevertheless, campaigns for justice which draw on human rights standards and make reference to the treaties to which a country has signed up can be effective. So for example, campaigns to address the issue of exploitative child labour have achieved success in this way.

The challenge today is to ensure that the international human rights standards agreed since World War II are known and understood. Even when individuals are aware of these standards, this knowledge needs to be accompanied by mechanisms which enable practical redress, and by a commitment to promote human rights as principles for living together.

We are conscious of a worldwide movement of people working towards the recognition and protection of human rights, particularly the human rights of the most marginalised and vulnerable. Over a number of years we have learned a great deal from scholars, NGO activists, and from those who have taken part in training courses we have led. *Teachers and Human Rights Education* is a contribution to the development of education in human rights in schools. We hope it will be useful to teachers, and to those who work with them, in helping to build a stronger culture of human rights among those who are responsible for educating children and young people.

The structure of this book

In *Teachers and Human Rights Education*, we confront many of the tensions and questions which arise when educators seek to introduce or develop programmes to promote human rights education in schools in a range of international contexts. We build upon our previous book on human rights education (Osler and Starkey, 1996), presenting our more recent experiences and research in this field.

The book is divided into three parts. In the current Part One *Human Rights: an Agenda for Action*, the three narratives in this chapter are followed in chapter two by a contextualisation of human rights education (HRE), a brief presentation of developments in HRE and some reflections on our own engagement in this area of work. Chapter three examines human rights from historical, sociological and legal perspectives, and chapter four considers human rights as a vision of peace and justice in the world, making the case for human rights education.

In Part Two we consider *Politics, Cultures and Inequalities*. Chapter five, on women's human rights, reflects on the meaning of the term 'women's human rights'; examines why human rights frameworks have often failed to meet the needs of half the world's population; and presents human rights as a project in progress, rather than as a fixed or unchangeable legal framework. Arguing that recognition of women's human rights has considerable and complex implications for an understanding of human rights more generally, it considers how racial, economic and gender privilege do not operate independently but together. It explores how a human rights framework can illuminate these processes. Chapter six considers the relationship between human rights and development, examining these in the context of globalisation. Chapter seven focuses on the relationships between values, cultures and human rights, examining the concerns of critics that universal rights undermine cultural specificities and that agreed common standards are not possible within multicultural societies. We consider the debates surrounding human rights values, universality, and cultural relativism and how these issues are understood both internationally and in the context of multicultural nation-states.

In the final Part Three we explore the practice of *Human Rights and Democracy in Schools*. Chapter eight focuses on children's human rights, examining changing conceptions of childhood. It considers how recognition of children's human rights requires us to re-think many of the established practices of schooling. Chapter nine focuses on the relationship between human rights education and citizenship education, since citizenship education is often posited by governments as the area of the school curriculum which encompasses human rights. We argue that citizenship education, as it is most commonly perceived, is an inadequate vehicle for human rights education, yet it is possible to reconceptualise citizenship and citizenship education more inclusively; underpinned by international human rights principles.

Finally, in chapter ten we propose some pedagogical principles for human rights education and discuss some of the challenges of introducing human rights education into imperfect school systems where issues such as competition, inequalities, and authoritarian and violent structures remain. *Teachers and Human Rights Education* closes with an epilogue. Here we return to the narratives introduced in this chapter. We consider the significance of these narratives for teachers as human rights educators.

The consideration of human rights does not provide us with neat answers to the many challenges, both educational and political, faced by schools, local communities, nations and the international community. In some ways this book raises more questions than it answers. The aim is to provide an internationally recognised framework for dialogue in addressing key issues of justice and equality. This framework recognises the complexities of human experience and permits us to address the intersectionality of injustices and inequalities and the multiple and complex ways in which individuals experience racism, sexism and injustices relating to poverty and structural disadvantage. This book examines how human rights education might be developed as an agenda for action in working for justice and peace in the world. It is a modest contribution to an on-going dialogue.

2

Contextualising human rights

Across the globe, governments have made commitments to both human rights and to human rights education. Yet, in many cases, such commitments are not backed by effective public awareness initiatives or appropriate professional development opportunities. Teachers, parents and educational policy-makers may be unclear about the precise nature of these commitments or their relevance to the day-to-day lives of both teachers and learners.

In Britain, as in a number of other countries, radio and TV news bulletins increasingly make explicit reference to human rights. Such news items include local and national concerns, on the one hand, and questions of international significance, on the other. They address matters as diverse as care of the elderly; access to new medical treatments; transport infrastructure; criminal justice; conflicts or natural disasters; child poverty; and global terrorism. Campaigners, politicians and the media regularly cite human rights to justify or challenge actions that range from peaceful protest to military action. The phrase 'human rights' sometimes appears to have become a slogan in need of a definition.

Despite this increasing use of human rights rhetoric, we have observed a widespread lack of familiarity with human rights instruments among educators in a number of countries. Many people know of the Universal Declaration of Human Rights 1948 (UDHR), but unless they have a legal background, or went to school in a country where the UDHR featured prominently in the curriculum, they are often unable to clarify its status or provide an overview of its content. In the UK, where we both live, it is quite common for journalists to confuse international human rights instruments, not realising, for example, that there are significant differences between declarations, conventions and covenants and that there are mechanisms designed to monitor and support nation-states in meeting specific human rights obligations. Rather than emphasise that human rights belong to us all, some newspapers give the impression that human rights are claimed only by celebrities or law-breakers, either frivolously or to avoid responsibility and criminal justice.

Across the 47 member-states of the Council of Europe, individuals (both citizens and non-citizens) are protected by the European Convention on Human Rights 1950 (ECHR). If they believe their rights have been infringed and they fail to secure redress in the national courts, they may appeal to the European Court of Human Rights, in Strasbourg, France. Yet before an individual seeks redress, she first needs to be aware that she has specific human rights, as well as know the means by which she can claim those rights. Human rights education is thus an essential element in guaranteeing human rights. Human rights education strengthens human rights across the globe and gives human rights their potency. A right is not an effective right unless you know about it.

Unfortunately, some sixty years on from the drafting of the Universal Declaration of Human Rights, the record of nation-states in guaranteeing citizens access to human rights education is extremely mixed. The popular confusions which surround many aspects of human rights seem to multiply when we focus on human rights education. Teachers and other education professionals are usually aware that there is a right to education, but fewer teachers and learners are clear about the right to human rights education or what precisely it might mean.

Our aims

Teachers and Human Rights Education has an ambitious agenda. The aim is not only to clarify the relevance of human rights to teachers' everyday work, but also to situate human rights education within a wider political context. We analyse human rights as an agenda for action. We contend that the realisation of children's human rights implies considerable changes in the organisation and structures of schooling, most notably changes which give young people opportunities to express their views and to have these views taken into consideration in the design of education services.

A further aim is to examine critically the focus of much current human rights education in schools. Human rights are a means for holding governments to account and for defending the interests of those individuals and groups who are marginalised or denied access to power, including children. From this perspective it becomes clear that a module on human rights within a citizenship education course, or a couple of lessons on children's rights, cannot be construed as addressing young people's entitlement to human rights education.

The emphasis in those school programmes that address children's human rights is usually on the horizontal relations between individuals. This neglects the vertical relationship between the individual and the nation-state. Students who follow such lessons are not usually made aware of the responsibility of the government to uphold the rights of all, or the means by which they might hold governments, particularity their own government, to account when their rights, or those of others, are infringed. We contend that this is an essential element of human rights education.

Human rights are sometimes presented as a project which has been fully realised. Children may be taught about the principles of the equal dignity of all humanity; of universality of rights; and of non-discrimination. Yet they will know from their knowledge of recent history and of the contemporary world, that political realities are a long way from these ideals. War and conflict, hunger and suffering persist. Children and young people are also likely to be aware that the gap between the ideals of human rights and their own everyday realities is immense.

Human rights need to be critically examined in the context of these realities and their potential as tools for change and transformation explored. Young people need to understand that these ideals have rarely, if ever, been achieved without struggle. Human rights education cannot simply be about ideals. Young people need to test human rights as tools for change and transformation and to understand their strengths and limitations. The ongoing struggle for women's human rights demonstrates that human rights are not a body of unchanging laws, but are developing and being re-interpreted in our own times.

Although many governments claim to provide human rights education, we argue that what passes for human rights education in many policy documents and schools is, at best, inadequate, and may be little more than a mechanism for managing young people's behaviour. Some of what is designated human rights education is designed to encourage compliance amongst learners, rather than to promote critical thinking. Young children may be taught simply to be nice to each other, rather than to stand up for justice. Among all age groups, this approach may entail encouraging peer censure of those who engage in disruptive behaviour and fail to respect the rights of fellow students in the classroom.

Teachers and Human Rights Education aims to contribute to the process of developing a human rights pedagogy for schools. In doing so, we give particular emphasis to the perspectives and insights of the marginalised and those engaged in struggles for justice and equality. Human rights education implies a deeper understanding of human rights principles; the encouragement of commitment to social justice and solidarity with those whose rights are denied; the development of critical thinking skills; and skills to effect change.

Another aim is to examine the strengths and limitations of human rights as a framework for living together in communities characterised by diversity. The processes of globalisation mean that students are increasingly likely to live and work alongside others from different social and cultural backgrounds, who do not necessarily share the same beliefs or values. Not all students will be citizens of the country in which they are living. It is no longer appropriate, if it ever was, to draw on a singular national, cultural or religious tradition in order to establish a framework of principles for living and working together in the community of the school or to prepare students for living in the wider communities they will encounter beyond school. *Teachers and Human Rights Education* examines human rights as a basis for dialogue between differing perspectives and as principles for living together and resolving conflicts justly and peaceably.

A linked aim is to consider the role of human rights and human rights education in enabling the development of successful multicultural democracies. In many multicultural democracies, the ideal of guaranteeing all members of the society equal access to educational opportunities, employment, justice, and many goods and services is far from being realised. Even when formal political equality exists, there remain barriers, including racism, sexism and poverty, which prevent individuals and groups from participating on the basis of equality. We consider the challenges facing teachers as human rights educators working in contexts of inequality, where the ideals promoted in international human rights instruments are in contrast to the gross inequalities experienced by young people.

We examine current practices in education for diversity and equality (often characterised as multicultural or intercultural education), mindful that migrant populations; other visible minorities; national, linguistic and religious minorities; and indigenous peoples are among those most vulnerable to racism and discrimination in many different national contexts. Of particular importance are those aspects of multicultural or intercultural education that address the skills and attitudes of mainstream populations.

This book is written for education professionals and researchers, particularly, but not exclusively, those concerned with the formal sector, with schools and with teacher education. In a few countries and schools there is a timetabled subject of human rights education, but in many contexts the governmental commitment, sometimes expressed as a clear policy goal, is to implement human rights education across the curriculum. The established school subjects of civics, citizenship education and political education are often identified as the main means through which the nation-state will meet its commitment to provide human rights education. For this reason, we give special attention in this book to education for democratic citizenship.

Where we are coming from
A struggle for greater justice in Britain

It was during the mid 1980s that we both became interested in the potential of human rights and human rights education to contribute to a wider project of racial and social justice in Britain. Hugh was working in a teachers' college in Oxford and Audrey was a member of a city-wide team of advisory teachers in Birmingham, working collaboratively with teachers in their classrooms to develop the school curriculum. Although Audrey's post had an explicit anti-racist brief, and Birmingham was among one of a number of English local authorities engaging in innovative policy and curriculum development, this was a decade when it became increasingly difficult and even controversial to engage in antiracist education.

It was the Thatcher era, in which national education policy became marked by a focus on the free market, restricted public spending and an emphasis on traditional knowledge and moral values. Teachers and teacher training were under attack from government and work on equalities was presented as a distraction from the core purposes of schooling. The British government was overtly antagonistic to antiracism in education and other policy areas, with the Prime Minister arguing that alien cultures were swamping Britain (Gilroy, 1987). There was continuing debate about immigration and British nationality and increasing social, racial and economic divisions. In 1981 there had been serious rioting in a number of cities, notably Toxteth in Liverpool, Brixton in London and Handsworth in Birmingham.

Early in 1985, the Swann Report *Education for All* (1985) was published, which advocated a multicultural education for all students, including those from white communities. Although a number of local education authorities had already established multicultural, antiracist and equal opportunities policies in the late 1970s and early 1980s, following Swann such initiatives multiplied and by the end of the decade two thirds of authorities had developed such policies (Tomlinson, 2008). The tensions existing between a number of progressive local authorities and the Conservative government left a small space in which educators could continue to work for greater social justice and equality.

In September 1985, as we were preparing to attend a conference on human rights education in Denmark supported by the Council of Europe, there was further rioting in the Handsworth and Lozells areas of Birmingham. Two Asian men died when their post office was set alight, in the midst of widespread destruction, burning and looting. A few days after the riots, Audrey visited a primary school in Lozells, where children were sitting in complete silence, drawing and writing about what they had seen and heard. She took some of their work to Denmark, but was shocked to find that some colleagues there believed that racial tensions and even riots were the inevitable outcome of a multicultural society.

In 1988 an Education Reform Act was passed which abolished the largest, inner London local authority and, by centralised control of funding and curriculum, reduced the influence of other local authorities. Effectively, much of the curriculum development designed to support gender and race equality and human rights was undermined or curtailed. Our work in human rights education began with us believing that by naming our antiracist initiatives as 'human rights education' we would avoid much of the official hostility that was undermining the effectiveness of such work with teachers in Britain. After all, we figured, what government would want to be seen as opposing human rights?

In 1986, Hugh brought together a small group of people working in teacher education, local authorities and in non-governmental organisations (NGOs) and local education authorities to discuss the formation of an *Education in Human Rights Network* (EIHRN). The Network, of which we were both founder members, operated from 1987-2001 and, building on the work of the Council of Europe and efforts to promote human rights education in other European countries, aimed to promote human rights education in Britain. EIHRN members met twice a year, sharing information, organising conferences, and sponsoring publications.

An important feature of EIHRN was that it promoted collaboration between educators and human rights lawyers. It enjoyed, in particular, the support of Kevin Boyle of the Centre for Human Rights at the University of Essex. The 1996 summer school, which took place in Derry, Northern Ireland, enabled us to begin developing valuable cooperative relationships with colleagues in both Northern Ireland and the Republic of Ireland. From the late 1990s, EIHRN, in collaboration with Amnesty International UK, secured funding to produce a series of materials which aimed to support those teaching human rights and citizenship in secondary schools through a range of subjects, including modern languages, history and mathematics (Brown, 2002a and 2002b; Brown and Slater, 2002; Wright, 2004).

Equally importantly, EIHRN engaged in a series of lobbying activities. In 1997, when the UK government's advisory group on citizenship published its first draft report (QCA, 1998b) as part of the process of introducing citizenship education as a subject on the national curriculum for England. We invited the Chair, Bernard Crick, to a EIHRN teachers' conference in Birmingham to engage in dialogue on the place of human rights within the citizenship curriculum. There were no references to human rights in this draft report. We argued that human rights needed to underpin the new citizenship curriculum. Although the final report did not go this far, it mentioned some key human rights instruments (QCA, 1998a) and subsequent curriculum guidance for schools has strengthened the place of human rights within the citizenship curriculum (QCA and DfES, 2001a and b; QCA and DCSF 2007a and b).

At the same time, we worked to raise the profile of human rights education within initial and continuing teacher education. In 1992, Audrey established a masters' programme in Education for Human Rights and Equality at the University of Birmingham and in 1998 she received an award from the Economic and Social Research Council (ESRC) to fund a series of research seminars on the theme of Human Rights and Democracy in Schools. A number of papers from this group were published as *Citizenship and Democracy in Schools* (Osler, 2000a). This book has become a popular text in initial teacher education courses.

From 1999, when Audrey was appointed to a Chair at the University of Leicester, the university's Centre for Citizenship Studies in Education (CCSE) became the focus for our collaboration on human rights education. It was here that we conducted the initial research on the theory and practice of education for cosmopolitan citizenship, based on human rights principles (Osler and Vincent, 2002; Osler and Starkey, 2003 and 2005). We also recorded teachers' accounts of human rights practice (Osler, 2005c). At CCSE, Hugh set up one of the first courses in citizenship education, introduced into the national curriculum for England in 2002. This course applied human rights principles to the teaching of citizenship, and drew directly on our developing research on education for cosmopolitan citizenship which, we argue, can be understood from a range of spatial perspectives, from the local to the global.

From 2004, when we moved to the universities of London and Leeds, we have contributed to the continuing professional development of teachers by offering short courses, supported by the Ministry of Education in England, and targeted at teachers and local authority officers, to support the implementation of citizenship education programmes and strengthen human rights education in schools.

Nevertheless we remain concerned about the fragile nature of such initiatives within the framework of initial teacher education and continuing professional development of teachers. At universities, professional development programmes for teachers continue to focus on school management and leadership, whereas initial teacher education focuses on core skills and competencies. Courses in human rights, participation and learning to live together are either marginal or non-existent in these programmes. A meeting of human rights education stakeholders which met in September 2009 at the European Union Agency for Fundamental Rights (FRA) in Vienna reported that this pattern is repeated across a number of European Union member-states. Countries like Spain which give human rights a stronger curriculum focus are the exception rather than the rule.

International collaboration

In 2008, the National Union of Teachers (NUT), in cooperation with the National Education Association (NEA) in the United States began a modest programme of human rights education for members. World Teachers' Day, held annually on 5 October since 1994, commemorates the anniversary of the signing in 1966 of the UNESCO/International Labour Organisation (ILO) Recommendation Concerning the Status of Teachers. It is an occasion to celebrate the essential role of teachers in providing quality education at all levels. World Teachers' Day 2009 put the spotlight on the global teacher shortage and the challenge of being a teacher today. UNESCO (2009) observed:

> In our rapidly changing and interdependent world, teachers not only have to ensure that students acquire solid skills in basic subjects, but also that they become responsible local and global citizens, at ease with new technologies and able to make informed decisions about health, the environment and other challenges.

UNESCO adds that while the global economic slowdown risks putting tight constraint on education budgets 'it is critical that governments support the recruitment, training and professional development of teachers'.

We would add that to meet the challenge of *quality* universal primary education, it is equally important that the training and professional development of these teachers must necessarily address human rights and gender equity. The Millennium Development Goals (MDGs) include the requirement that: 'by 2015, children everywhere, boys and girls alike, will be able to complete a full course of primary schooling'. It is broadly recognised that quality is as important as enrolment. The goal of universal primary education is matched by one on promoting gender equality and empowering women. The MGD target is: 'Eliminate gender disparity in primary and secondary education, preferably by 2005, and in all levels of education no later than 2015'. As Unterhalter (2008) has observed, these goals have been interpreted by some countries in a minimalist way, simply to mean 'get girls into school'. The realisation of women's and girls' human rights requires a commitment to the development of schools in which gender equality and human rights are recognised and valued. This implies human rights education for both teachers and students and the transformation of schools into rights respecting institutions. Addressing human rights in the training and professional development of school administrators, planners and teachers are critical steps in realising quality education for all.

Our understanding of human rights education has been greatly enhanced through a number of international collaborations. Through the 1990s we led the English language strand of a summer school hosted by a Geneva-based NGO *Association mondiale pour l'école instrument de paix* (World Association of School as an Instrument for Peace) (EIP), which brought together teachers from Africa, Asia, Latin America, North America, and Europe in a large annual summer school focusing on a human rights education theme. In 1991, Hugh secured European Commission funds to establish a Europe-wide network to develop teacher education curricula which were designed to ensure that new entrants to teaching are equipped to encourage global and intercultural perspectives and contribute to 'the safeguarding of the principles of democracy, social justice and respect for human rights'. This project enabled participants to visit each others' institutions and to promote student exchanges. Among its many outcomes were two books (Osler, Rathenow and Starkey,1996; Holden and Clough, 1998).

The Council of Europe has also supported our work in this area, with two edited books, the first focusing specifically on human rights education (Starkey, 1991) and the second examining human rights, development and global perspectives (Osler, 1994a). The Council also supported the publication of *Teacher Education and Human Rights* (Osler and Starkey, 1996). Other significant projects which have impacted on our understandings have been a human rights education initiative which Audrey undertook with colleagues in Ethiopia between 1992 and 1994 supported by the Carter Center at Emory University Atlanta, Georgia; her visits to Taiwan to engage in human rights education (1998 and 2004); a British Council funded project with the University of Western Cape, South Africa 2001-04, in which we were both involved; and our visits to Korea in 2006 and 2007, sponsored by the Korean National Commission for Human Rights, the Korean Ministry of Education and the UK Foreign Office. Each of the above projects has focused largely on the integration of human rights principles and practices into the school curriculum and/or teacher education.

Since 2001, we have also had extended opportunities to engage in discussion and debate on human rights education with a range of colleagues in Canada and in the USA. From 2001, a group of human rights education scholars and activists brought together by Nancy Flowers of Amnesty International USA worked together to extend their understandings of human rights education, beginning by planning and leading a workshop on human rights education and antiracism at the 2001 UN Conference against Racism in Durban, South Africa. Audrey was privileged to be part of that group. From 2003 to 2005 Audrey was also a member of a Diversity, Citizenship, and Global Education Panel convened by James A. Banks of the University of Washington, Seattle, which set out to identify key principles and concepts that teachers might use to develop or renew citizenship education programmes which address unity and diversity. The panel concluded that:

> The teaching of human rights should underpin citizenship education courses and programs in multicultural nation-states. (Banks *et al*, 2005)

We believe there is growing evidence from around the world which supports this principle and this book is premised upon it. Yet this idea, while not controversial in Canada, remains quite challenging in the United States.

Since 2004, our scholarship in human rights education has continued at the University of Leeds, in the Centre for Citizenship and Human Rights Education, which Audrey founded, and at the Institute of Education, University of London where Hugh is co-director of the International Centre for Education for Democratic Citizenship. Audrey established an interdisciplinary masters' programme in Education and Democracy in Leeds, and Hugh developed an online masters' programme in Citizenship and History Education in London, both of which have attracted British and international students. Both programmes are underpinned by human rights principles.

We continue to be encouraged by the work of colleagues working in NGOs and in international organisations. In 1994 human rights education was placed on the United Nations agenda with the launch of the UN Decade for Human Rights Education, largely as the result of efforts by Shulamith Koenig and the People's Decade for Human Rights Education. Although the end of the Decade saw only modest efforts by governmental bodies to develop action plans to implement human rights education, the UN agreed to follow it by the World Programme for Human Rights Education which was proclaimed on 10 December 2004.

At the end of the first phase in 2009, just thirteen member-states have developed action plans on HRE and a further fourteen have references to HRE within their overall action plans on human rights (OHCHR, 2009). During the decade and since, an international networking organisation, Human Rights Education Associates (HREA), has enabled effective communication and resource sharing among human rights educators across the globe. At the time of writing, a draft UN Declaration on Human Rights Education and Training is under consultation and is expected to be approved in 2010.

3

Human rights frameworks

Human rights provide a way of looking at the world. The three narratives presented in chapter one can be read both as individual stories and as personal accounts which illustrate wider injustice and suffering. When nation-states fail to take action to protect individuals or groups in their territories; when they discriminate against groups on the basis of ethnicity; or when they carelessly fail to take a course of action to alleviate suffering or protect health; they undermine both the dignity of those populations and their status as persons, challenging their very humanity. Since the Universal Declaration of Human Rights (UDHR) 1948 we have a shared language to describe and name ways in which human dignity may be violated.

As Yoriko's story illustrates, when the US government interned some 110,000 people during World War II, two thirds of whom were citizens, the rest being mostly long-term residents ineligible for naturalisation, this action devastated the lives of Japanese-Americans (CWRIC, [1983] 1996). When families and communities were divided and cultural traditions damaged, they lost their livelihoods and economic independence, as well as their emotional security. Their dignity was taken away as traditional self-reliance was replaced by forced dependence on the nation-state. The very basis of human rights is an understanding that 'human dignity is especially vulnerable to state threats and actions' Eddy (2007:325). The internment of Japanese Americans took place before there was an international consensus on human rights. However, a human rights perspective motivated a struggle lasting four decades for recognition of the wrong perpetrated by the nation-state. The campaigners received an official apology in 1987.

What Esmé experienced in Singapore was the British army evacuating white civilians as the Japanese Imperial Army advanced but failing to offer protection to non-white civilians in the colony. These British subjects underwent acute suffering and many lost their lives, as the result of an official decision to abandon them; effectively discrimination by ethnicity. This was typical of the colonial policies of the British government at that time. Today, we can use the language of human rights to identify and describe policies and administrative decisions that are based on ethnic discrimination.

The third story, told by an unnamed teacher, is of a young woman, Leleti, who suffers violent abuse at the hands of her husband, and who encounters difficulty in accessing the medical care and drugs she needs to fight HIV AIDS. Her story takes place in South Africa, where there was for a number of years official denial of the pandemic and a consequent difficulty among the poor in accessing appropriate treatments.

It is not just the nation-state that operates to infringe rights. A gender-neutral approach to human rights has long meant that specific human rights abuses like domestic violence, to which women are especially vulnerable, have gone unaddressed. Leleti's security, dignity and ultimately her very life are lost as her rights are infringed. She is wronged both by the state and by her own husband. The government was arguably not directly responsible for the failure to meet her basic needs, but it failed to meet 'the state's overarching duty to respect the dignity of its citizens and their status as beings of equal human worth' (Eddy, 2007:325).

Each of the stories told in chapter one recalls situations that we now recognise as human rights violations, since in every case the nation-state (and others) failed to respect the dignity of the young woman concerned (and that of many other women, men and children in their families and communities). The nation-state (and others) also failed to respect their status as beings of equal worth.

We can draw on human rights to read these stories and to read the world. Human rights provide a lens through which we can critically examine situations and events. By beginning the process of defining universal human rights in 1948, the United Nations, the one body representing the entire global community, provided a language that all can use to demand active protection of our lives and freedoms by state authorities; to describe and identify oppression and inequality; and to claim solidarity with others in struggles for rights.

A human rights perspective gave weight to the cause of those Japanese-Americans who suffered at the hands of their government. A human rights perspective persuaded President Carter to set up the commission of inquiry.

It was this human rights perspective that eventually allowed their fellow citizens to see the justice of their cause. The commission's report *Personal Justice Denied* (CWRIC, [1983] 1996) concluded that the imprisonment of Japanese citizens and residents was a 'grave injustice' which resulted from 'race prejudice, war hysteria, and a failure of political leadership'.

This chapter proposes various theoretical and disciplinary frameworks that may help educators to engage critically with human rights. Human rights can be studied from many disciplinary perspectives; historical, legal, sociological, moral, philosophical and political amongst others, all of which overlap and mingle. Nation-states have accepted that they have an obligation to ensure that their populations have an understanding of human rights. Teachers have a vital role in helping to fulfil this undertaking. Rather than present lists of rights for memorisation, we need to engage critically with students to examine the underlying principles of human rights and apply them to everyday living.

Whilst there is no agreement on the status of attempts to develop a general theory of human rights (Turner, 1993; Douzinas, 2000), a human rights perspective enables us to understand and interrogate many aspects of human interactions, including those involving the state and its institutions. The development of human rights occurred because human beings felt the need, in the light of human vulnerability, for agreement on moral, political and legal principles that might protect individuals.

The principles are abstract and can thus be applied to any context and in any political system. They recognise that human beings live in society and depend on others for their survival and well-being. These standards provide a common point of reference for teachers and educators as they engage with students from a wide diversity of cultural, ethnic and religious backgrounds. Schools can help to ensure that human rights are known and understood, not simply as normative standards for encouraging pro-social behaviour, but also as a set of principles for critically engaging with social and political realities.

Human rights: historical perspectives

As Gertrude Stein (1924) wrote: 'Let me recite what history teaches. History teaches'. The study of events, actions and movements that make up the history of human rights informs the present. Historical questions relating to human rights include: why universal rights were developed in the mid-twentieth century (Klug, 2000; Glendon, 2001; Borgwardt, 2005; Winter, 2006); how the texts and instruments that define these rights affect the behaviours of governments and individuals (Cassese, 1990; Douzinas, 2000; Nash, 2009); and how the concept of human rights developed from previous struggles for freedom (Ishay, 2004; Hunt, 2007; Ashley, 2008). In this section we focus on the great human achievement that is the text of the Universal Declaration of Human Rights (UDHR). We set the drafting process in the historical context of World War II and the founding of the United Nations; examine the conceptual basis of the UDHR; outline some of the struggles over the text; assess some steps that were taken to strengthen its claims to universality; and provide examples that illustrate its significance.

Waves of rights

Human rights are often spoken of from a historical perspective as having developed in three generations or waves (Klug, 2000). This categorisation is sometimes contested as being in tension with the notion of indivisibility of rights, but it can serve to remind us of historic struggles (Bowring, 2008). First wave rights are those civil and political rights necessary for meaningful citizenship. They are associated with the Enlightenment and with struggles for freedom from the arbitrary and unjust actions of colonial powers and of monarchs claiming the divine right to rule. Exemplary historic declarations, asserting equality of rights and the right of subjects to rebel against tyranny, are the United States Declaration of Independence 1776 and the French revolutionary Declaration of the Rights of Man and of the Citizen 1789. The historical significance of the declarations is recognised in twentieth century declarations and covenants through the use of phrases and formulations drawn directly from them. Interestingly, it has been argued that one explanation for the absence of plans for reconstruction following the military invasions of Afghanistan in 2001 and Iraq in 2003 can be traced to a historically constituted US mindset that the defeat of tyranny is an end in itself (Gray, 2007).

The second wave of human rights is associated with social and economic rights. These rights are included in the UDHR and they have their origins in trade union struggles from the nineteenth century. They were first elaborated through the International Labour Organisation (ILO) whose 1919 constitution contains an explicit commitment to social justice that has been a key principle in international law ever since (Brownlie, 1971; Bowring, 2008).

Third wave rights are sometimes called solidarity rights. They are associated with major struggles of the post-World War II period: decolonisation; development; peace; and environmental protection. Whilst the rights invoked for these struggles are not new, powerful international campaigns, often led by non-governmental organisations (NGOs) have achieved a series of instruments, declarations, covenants and guidelines that commit the world community to global solidarity. Third wave rights add to and build on the struggles of previous generations, but do not replace them. Struggles for civil and political rights and for social and economic rights remain on the agenda alongside efforts to realise sustainable development.

Cassin's conception of human rights

The metaphor of generations or waves of rights tends to emphasise the difference between groups of rights rather than their interdependence and indivisibility. One of the key drafters of the UDHR, René Cassin, proposed an alternative model that presents four groups of rights as pillars, holding up an edifice of internationally agreed human rights (Figure 3.1). Each pillar helps support the edifice of the UDHR, imagined as a classical Greek portico, and each bears equal weight.

The foundations of the portico are the preamble and the first article, a statement of belief in what has developed as natural rights theory, namely that 'all human beings are born free and equal in dignity and rights'. This is followed by a normative statement of how people should behave towards each other. 'They are endowed with reason and conscience and should act towards one another in a spirit of brotherhood'. The formulation consciously echoes the American and French Declarations from the eighteenth century.

The pillars of the UDHR portico symbolise four key concepts, namely dignity, liberty, equality and solidarity, the last three recognisable as the motto of the French Republic. Cassin clusters the articles as: personal rights; rights in civil society; public freedoms and political rights; and economic, social and cultural rights. The pediment capping the edifice represents an international order essential for the realisation of rights; understanding that rights imply duties to the community; and a recognition that freedoms do not extend to those actions that jeopardise the rights of others.

The UDHR introduced a new concept of universality. Previous struggles established citizenship rights guaranteed at national level. The essence of human rights, as expressed in the UDHR, is that they are *universal* and not the gifts of national governments. The President of the UN General Assembly 1948, which proclaimed the UDHR, observed that this was 'the first occasion on which the organised world community had recognised the existence of human rights and fundamental freedoms transcending the laws of sovereign states' (Laqueur and Rubin, 1979:1).

Articles 28-30			
an international order for the realisation of rights			
Articles 2-11	**Articles 12-17**	**Articles 18-21**	**Articles 22-27**
Life, liberty, personal security	Rights in civil society	Political rights and freedoms	Economic, social and cultural rights
	Privacy		
Equality of rights	Movement in out of country	Belief and religion	Social security
No torture		Opinion and information	Work and trade unions
No slavery	Asylum	Peaceful assembly	Rest and leisure
Equality before law	Nationality		
	Marriage	Democracy	Adequate living standard
Fair trial due process	Property		
			Education
			Cultural life
DIGNITY	LIBERTY	EQUALITY	SOLIDARITY

Preamble and Article 1: equality of dignity and the rights of all – the foundations of freedom, justice and peace

Figure 3.1: Cassin's model of the UDHR

Struggles to influence the Charter of the United Nations
The Charter of the United Nations, signed in San Francisco on 26 June 1945 by representatives of 51 nation-states, is explicitly based on a determination to draw lessons from the catastrophic events of a specific historical period 1914-1945. It aims to: 'save succeeding generations from the scourge of war, which twice in our lifetime has brought untold sorrow to mankind' (UNO, 1945).

Discussions on the principles for a post-war settlement were set in train at a 1941 wartime meeting between British Prime Minister Winston Churchill and US President Franklin D. Roosevelt. A communiqué, now known as the Atlantic Charter, was issued proposing eight 'common principles' to define a world order worth fighting for. These included recognition of 'the right of all peoples to choose the form of government under which they live' including the restoration of self-government. Roosevelt is quoted as saying: 'I can't believe that we can fight a war against fascist slavery, and at the same time not work to free people all over the world from a backward colonial policy' (Ishay, 2004:180). Although committed to the continuation of the British Empire, Churchill was obliged to agree to this form of words and this immediately raised expectations amongst those struggling against colonial oppression.

The Atlantic Charter also included the principle that 'all the men [sic] in all lands may live out their lives in freedom from fear and want'. The first part of this phrase was revolutionary in implying that the well-being and dignity of individuals were now the legitimate concern of international diplomacy, rather than nation-states. Once in the public sphere, this idea 'was soon to catalyse groups around the world committed to fighting colonialism and racism as well as Nazism' (Borgwardt, 2005:4).

In January 1942, just after the USA had entered the war, four major powers, US, USSR, China and UK and 22 other nation-states signed the Declaration of the United Nations, based on the eight principles of the Atlantic Charter. This Declaration explicitly introduced the concept of human rights to international diplomatic discourse, justifying the war in terms of preserving 'human rights and justice'. Over the next three years the United Nations became an organisation.

The UN Charter sets out mechanisms and organisational arrangements based on the equality within the organisation of 'nations large and small'. This is represented and symbolised in the UN General Assembly, a periodic meeting to which all members are invited to send delegates. Underpinning this apparatus is a set of beliefs including, significantly: 'faith in fundamental human rights, in the dignity and worth of the human person, in the equal rights of men and women'.

A commitment to human rights and gender equality was not included in the initial draft of the UN Charter. In the 1944 negotiations, the UK attempted to protect its empire where many fundamental rights were denied to local populations. The USSR similarly wished to avoid constraints to its state interests. When China proposed a statement on the equality of all races, this was opposed by the USA (Hunt, 2007).

Concern for the rights of peoples living under colonial governments motivated many nation-states involved in the UN Charter negotiations. Observing the convenors of the San Francisco meeting (USA, USSR, China and UK) retreating from universal principles of equality, Australia, New Zealand, India, the Philippines and Latin American states demanded explicit commitments to human rights in the new Charter. Powerful NGOs such as the World Trade Union Congress and the Provisional World Council of Dominated Nations added their weight as many resistance leaders, including Mahatma Gandhi, Carlos Romulo, Ho Chi Minh, Kwame Nkrumah and W.E.B. Dubois, condemned the inadequacies of the proposed text (Ishay, 2004). The convening nation-states were forced to give way. A strong and explicit commitment to human rights and gender equality was included in the Charter, though no commitment to democracy was made (De Baets, 2009).

This illustrates how those with less power can seize a human rights principle, once articulated, and use it to make strong political claims. The struggle over the UN Charter and the resultant recognition by colonial powers of the equal humanity of colonial peoples was highly significant. Universal human rights are derived from the universal experience of oppression, though this has rarely been articulated in historical accounts (Nyamu-Musembi, 2005; Stammers, 2005).

Achieving consensus on universal human rights

One of the first tasks of the United Nations was to define human rights. A small planning group chaired by Eleanor Roosevelt was convened in April 1946 to start the process (Glendon, 2001). Under her leadership, the Commission called on philosophers, lawyers, academics and theologians from many different traditions to explore how various insights, traditions and beliefs might be synthesised to encapsulate fundamental standards and principles acceptable across the globe.

The UN Educational Scientific and Cultural Organisation (UNESCO), contributed to this process. A questionnaire about the essence of humanity and about relationships between individuals and governments was sent to philosophers around the world, identified as representing a range of cultural backgrounds. 70 detailed responses were received and the report concluded that it had found agreement that 'men and women, all over the world, have the right to live a life that is free from the haunting fear of poverty and insecurity' (Ishay, 2004:220).

The UN's Director of Human Rights, Canadian law professor John Humphrey, drafted a Declaration for the UN General Assembly with the support of a small committee consisting of Eleanor Roosevelt, Pen-Chung Chang of China as vice-chair, René Cassin of France, and Charles Malik of Lebanon. A broader committee of eighteen member nation-states received and discussed successive drafts. During two years of preparation the document went through seven major drafts, which were discussed at nearly 200 meetings (Glendon, 2001). The Universal Declaration of Human Rights (UDHR) was finally adopted by the UN General Assembly by 48 member states voting in favour and eight abstentions: South Africa, Saudi Arabia and six Soviet bloc nations. Consensus was achieved across geographical, religious and ideological lines by seeking agreement on *which* principles and which rights to include and avoiding discussion of *why* nations and interest groups supported the Declaration.

Conceptual innovation

The great conceptual innovation introduced in the UDHR was one theorised by Cassin, based on his experiences representing displaced World War I veterans in Europe (Winter, 2006). Veterans were being denied their rights because they did not hold formal citizenship status. Yet they were clearly members of the communities where they lived. He argued that domicile as well as citizenship should be a source of rights. In other words, rights attach to individuals, wherever they live; they are not the gift of the nation-state. Once rights are conceived as belonging to the individual as human being rather than as citizen of a nation-state, the concept of human rights is possible.

This theoretical position was accepted by the nation-state signatories to the UDHR. Despite this, individuals and groups continued to struggle to achieve these rights. The African National Congress (ANC) in apartheid South Africa drew strength from the UDHR. The ANC's Freedom Charter 1955 has a key section entitled All Shall Enjoy Equal Human Rights. In framing the struggle as one for human rights, the ANC was able to call on governments, UN agencies and NGOs from around the world to show solidarity with its campaign. Following the ANC's victory in South Africa's first democratic elections in 1994, the Republic adopted a new constitution explicitly founded on the UDHR.

The UDHR also inspired US civil rights leader Malcolm X who argued that civil rights activists would only succeed if they campaigned for human rights and presented their case to the whole world. When framed in terms of global solidarity rather than domestic citizenship rights, 'anybody, anywhere on this earth can become your ally' (Malcolm X, 1965 in Clark, 1992:175).

Legal perspectives

The UDHR was a performative act by the world's nations. It supported a vision of peace based on democracy and the rule of law and set a moral standard. However, declarations cannot in themselves protect vulnerable human beings; laws are also needed to enforce standards. State institutions need to respect human dignity and fundamental freedoms. Political and social activists mobilise to ensure that governments develop legal frameworks in line with their international commitments to human rights. Some 200 human rights instruments, including declarations, resolutions, guidelines, conventions, and covenants make up a body of international human rights law that needs to be translated into legal and policy instruments operative at the level of the nation-state (Morsink, 1999).

The most powerful instruments are conventions and covenants, since, under the Vienna Convention on the Law of Treaties (1980), signatory governments are legally bound to observe their provisions. They agree to respect, protect and fulfil human rights. In other words, they refrain from restricting rights (respect); ensure legal security for the enjoyment of human rights (protect); and put in place measures that promote human rights (fulfil).

The centrepiece of international human rights law is the International Bill of Human Rights, made up of the International Covenant on Civil and Political Rights (ICCPR) and the International Covenant on Economic, Social and Cultural Rights (ICESCR) and their two protocols, together with the UDHR. The International Bill of Rights came into force in 1976 and includes a somewhat cumbersome provision for individuals to petition the UN.

Groups historically subject to discrimination have demanded further legal measures to address specific issues, as have groups campaigning internationally for the abolition of gross state-sanctioned abuses of rights. The UN's regime of nine core instruments consists of the two Covenants together with

---

Each treaty has a committee of experts to monitor implementation. The committee is known by the acronym of the treaty (eg ICERD)

International Convention on the Elimination of All Forms of Racial Discrimination (ICERD) 1965

International Covenant on Civil and Political Rights (ICCPR) 1966

International Covenant on Economic, Social and Cultural Rights (ICESCR) 1966

Convention on the Elimination of All Forms of Discrimination against Women (CEDAW) 1979

Convention against Torture and Other Cruel, Inhuman or Degrading Treatment or Punishment (CAT) 1984

Convention on the Rights of the Child (CRC) 1989

International Convention on the Protection of the Rights of All Migrant Workers and Members of Their Families (ICRMW) 1990

Convention on the Rights of Persons with Disabilities (CRPD) 2006

International Convention for the Protection of All Persons from Enforced Disappearance (ICPPED) 2006

Figure 3.2: Legally-enforceable international human rights instruments

seven conventions. These cover: the human rights of women, children, migrants and persons with disabilities; and the elimination of racial discrimination, torture and enforced disappearances (Figure 3.2).

The UN's expert monitoring bodies, one for each treaty, assess the performance of nation-states against these standards. States submit a self-evaluation report once every four or five years and the appropriate committee comments on this in the light of other evidence received, particularly from civil society groups. There is no system of punishments or fines. The process depends instead on the moral force of international public scrutiny. Nation-states do engage with the process and generally attempt to avoid damage to their reputations as members of the international community.

European Convention on Human Rights (ECHR)

The most developed system of legal human rights protection exists in Europe under the European Convention on Human Rights and Fundamental Freedoms (ECHR) 1950. The ECHR provides legal protection for most of the civil and political rights within the UDHR. It covers all residents in the jurisdiction of the 47 member-states of the Council of Europe. States accept that they will not resort to torture or the death penalty; nor interfere with matters of conscience and belief, free expression, peaceful assembly, personal property, correspondence and choice of marriage partner; nor discriminate in guaranteeing these rights. Individuals can take their case to the European Court of Human Rights, which has powers to bring member-states to account and oblige them to change their legislation. In the UK the Human Rights Act 2000 obliges judges and government ministers to take account of the ECHR in drawing up and in administering the law, giving it a quasi-constitutional status.

The interaction of the ECHR with domestic law is an example of an increasingly important trend, namely the development of an intermestic field of law, providing for a creative interplay between international conventions and domestic legal frameworks. For example, in England, the Court of Appeal ruled in *Wood v Commissioner for Police of the Metropolis* [2009] EWCA Civ 414, that the Metropolitan Police had acted unlawfully in retaining photographs taken of an anti-arms trade campaigner as he was leaving the Annual General Meeting of arms fair sponsor Reed Elsevier plc. Since Wood was not charged with any offence, keeping the photographs on file was a breach of his right to privacy under Article 8. The police authority was ordered to destroy the photos and pay the legal costs. In this case, a campaigning NGO successfully used human rights law to assert the right to peaceful protest and political activity. Subsequently the European Court of Human Rights found a breach of Article 8 in a similar case relating to an earlier arms fair (Gillan and Quinton v. The United Kingdom, 12 January 2010). In this case the campaigners had been stopped and searched under anti-terrorism legislation when there was no ostensible reason to do so.

Former distinctions between the realms of national law and international law are breaking down as judges consider the human rights duties of the nation-state and its institutions when making judgements in domestic courts. National courts must provide justice for all residents irrespective of formal citizenship. It can be argued that domestic law is being re-framed in a cosmopolitan rather than purely national perspective. The core instruments of the UN human rights regime act as a still provisional and contested 'global constitution' (Nash, 2009:36), providing overarching principles to which judges in domestic courts must refer. The field of law is itself a site of struggle. Legislators make the law and judges interpret it, not always to the liking of governments. Lawyers acting for social movements constantly challenge governments and state authorities. Although the terms in which the law is debated are grounded in reason and rationality, there may be unexpected consequences from such legal decisions. Human rights are sometimes discredited in the popular imagination by media coverage of particular cases where human rights are presented as protecting criminals and celebrities rather than everyone. There is an urgent need for human rights education to be part of the standard professional training of journalists.

There has been a struggle between the UK government and judges on how to handle terrorist suspects who are not UK nationals. Judges insist on the application of human rights principles and obligations, namely equal treatment before the law for nationals and non-nationals. The ECHR bans the deportation of non-nationals to a situation of political persecution or torture. In the 2004 case of the Belmarsh detainees, judges, operating on legal principles, ordered terrorist suspects to be released, since they had been imprisoned without charge. Lord Hoffman argued that this was in conformity with the 'quintessentially British liberty' of freedom from arbitrary arrest which the ECHR had simply codified for the benefit of other nations with less established legal protections (Nash, 2009:97). The political consequence was the release of alleged terrorists into the community. The application of human rights law in the case of a few, supposedly dangerous, non-nationals was presented in the press as a threat to national security. In 2005, the UK government introduced new anti-terrorist legislation to circumvent human rights obligations. In addition, the Opposition proposed scrapping the Human Rights Act.

Human rights law protects the rights of teachers to access and disseminate information; to develop programmes of human rights education; and to be active citizens and members of associations and trade unions. Teachers also have specific obligations under the Convention on the Rights of the Child (CRC) for ensuring that young citizens in schools are in a position to access their human rights.

Sociological Perspectives

The building of international institutions and laws to protect and promote human rights is an impressive human achievement, but it is not without contradictions and deficiencies. Freeman (2002:99) argues that the 'task of the social science of human rights is to bring human-rights supporters back to reality'. In other words, social scientists critically interrogate what governments, NGOs and individuals actually do in the name of human rights or in violation of human rights.

The long-established human rights NGO, Amnesty International (AI), aims to close the gap between the rhetorical commitments of governments and the failures of those governments and their agencies (including police, military and judiciary) to uphold rights. AI researchers identify politically motivated arrests and verify claims as to the status of prisoners of conscience. They gather evidence to mobilise members and supporters in campaigns for release, invoking the moral duty of nation-states to respect human rights. AI has created its own bureaucracy and systems of regulation to ensure that its moral authority is not jeopardised (Clark, 2001). Ironically, the US government has used AI reports to support military interventions such as the first Iraq war (Power, 2001). AI itself has also been the subject of an anthropological study that critiqued the experience of its employees (Hopgood, 2006).

Using sociological concepts of human frailty and vulnerability, Turner (1993:489) develops a theory of human rights as 'social claims for institutionalised protection'. His theory seeks to explain the development of social structures and institutions intended to protect people from the dangers of ill-health, poverty and social exclusion. By framing demands for dignity and justice in terms of human frailty, Turner argues that 'moral communities are created that support the institution of rights'. People identify with and have sympathy for others who, like themselves, are vulnerable. However, the very state institutions designed to protect people may threaten human rights. Nation-states' concerns to protect citizens from terrorism have created bureaucratic and surveillance systems that conflict with fundamental freedoms and which also may have discriminatory outcomes. There is a continuous struggle to ensure that the power of the state is regulated and administered fairly and justly.

Sociological research offers examples, case studies and theoretical understandings that can inform campaigns, policy and public awareness. For example, a study of the life experiences of Indonesian women living in the Netherlands exposed the myth of their smooth assimilation into Dutch society, enabling its author to generate a theory of everyday racism (Essed, [1984] 2002). Her theoretical insights inform research and educational programmes aimed at combating racism.

Academic research can help campaigners (Apple, 2008). A coalition of activists and researchers working for the right to education of Dalit children in India first studied the international human rights conventions ratified by the government, as well as the rights of minorities under the national constitution. They then reviewed a number of empirical studies that demonstrated discrimination in accessing mid-day meals, textbooks, uniforms and even school places. Dalit children were segregated in classrooms and at mealtimes; the curriculum failed to include their experience; and many teachers openly expressed contempt for them (Vijapur, 2008). The campaigners thus demonstrated ways in which the law had failed this group.

These findings reflect patterns of ethnic and racial discrimination in a wide range of educational contexts (Banks, 2006; Richardson, 2007; Nieto and Bode, 2008; Au, 2009). Collectively such studies reveal both a pattern of institutionalised discrimination and a common agenda for action. Blatant disregard for human rights standards by state authorities invites groups fighting for justice to work in solidarity with others.

The realisation of human rights requires moral pressure that translates into political pressure. Comparative studies may help set benchmarks or possibly shame governments into action or restraint. Studies may assess differential access to education by quantifying levels of illiteracy. They may analyse prison populations by gender, race and class, revealing patterns of discrimination. Other studies may attempt to quantify particular instances of human rights abuses such as extra-judicial killings by agents of the state. While the quantification of gross human rights abuses is important, a greater challenge is to 'explain and understand why such patterns of abuse persist even though the world has witnessed a significant proliferation of human rights norms since the 1948 Universal Declaration' (Landman, 2006:146).

This chapter reviewed the historical question of why human rights norms and instruments developed. It has examined, from a legal perspective, the obligations to which nation-states commit when they sign and ratify human rights conventions, and noted some limitations of the law and some political tensions following legal judgements. Finally, it considered the sociological questions of why and how discriminations and abuses persist and how they can be addressed. All these perspectives also include philosophical, political and moral dimensions. Teachers require at least a basic understanding of human rights since this provides a way of looking at the world independent of ideology and religion. By grounding their moral authority in international standards and principles they can explain their actions independently of their own background or convictions.

Historical, legal and sociological frameworks enable a deeper understanding of human rights. They also permit a critical examination of their context, development, strengths and limitations in realising social justice within local, national and global communities.

4

Human rights, justice and peace

The Universal Declaration of Human Rights (UDHR) presents a vision of a peaceful world; the outcome of a struggle by humanity to implement justice. It offers an emancipatory manifesto, a set of shared principles for living together and an agenda for action developed in response to the repressive totalitarian ideologies of the mid-twentieth century. The realisation of this vision of justice and peace is a utopian project. This chapter examines in detail the content and underlying principles of the UDHR. It argues that human rights provide a world view and, more concretely, a discourse with which to critique and challenge current social and economic conditions. The utopian ideals of freedom, justice and peace in the world are discussed in opposition to unfettered state power that crushes human dignity and destroys the conditions for human flourishing. The UDHR looks forward and back. Its provisions can be read both as inspirational rhetoric and as realistic principles for opposing oppressive state practices (Bédarida, 1992; Kershaw, 1995). It provides a universal standard against which national laws and their application can be scrutinised.

UDHR as cosmopolitan vision

The preamble of the UDHR encapsulates its vision:

> recognition of the inherent dignity and of the equal and inalienable rights of all members of the human family is the foundation of freedom, justice and peace in the world.

This assertion owes much to the eighteenth century Enlightenment philosophy of Immanuel Kant. It introduces the concept of human dignity from which all human rights ultimately derive. Kant argued that since human beings are rational, individuals can decide whether to act morally or not. They follow the categorical imperative when they choose to act rationally and morally. They recognise other human beings as ends in themselves, rather than a means to an end. Human dignity therefore depends on the judgements and (in)actions of others. However, dignity is also inherent to human beings. It is not granted by rulers but is an essential quality of all human beings.

The vision of achieving justice and peace in the world through human rights is based not on science but on belief. This is not a religious, metaphysical or humanist belief. It is an assessment that governance structures enjoying the support of the people are likely to provide a stable basis for developing national societies which enable international co-operation rather than conflict over territory and resources. This approach is simultaneously pragmatic and idealistic. The same conclusion about the best approach to achieving justice and peace in the world might be reached through other belief systems. The major religions and humanist philosophies all share commitments to peace and social justice. All recognise human beings as embedded in social structures and having the capacity to exercise choices, including the choice to reject any belief system.

The UDHR preamble, quoted above, makes further reference to Kantian philosophy, namely cosmopolitanism. Human beings are conceptualised metaphorically as a family. There is thus a common bond tying all humanity together. This is reinforced in Article 1 which asserts:

> All human beings are born free and equal in dignity and rights. They are endowed with reason and conscience and should act towards one another in a spirit of brotherhood.

Behind the patriarchal expression 'spirit of brotherhood' is an attempt to define all humanity as family. We note that this use of language that excludes half of humanity persisted 160 years after Olympe de Gouges published her Declaration of the Rights of Woman in order to reveal assumptions behind the French Revolution's foundational declaration. By contrast, the metaphor of family, which might signify hierarchy, patriarchy and conflict, has rarely been critiqued in the context of human rights. Here the image of an idealised and egalitarian family of humanity is part of the utopia.

A cosmopolitan perspective finds antecedents in many religious traditions and in humanism. The Indian concept of *Vasudhaiva Kutumbakam* (World is Family) dates back five thousand years (Chaurasia, 2000:iii). It is also the basis of theistic religions, where humanity is portrayed as descended from a single ancestral couple, Adam and Eve, or conceptualised as sons and daughters of God. The pre-war *Humanist Manifesto*, signed by the educational philosopher, John Dewey, suggested that humanism developed in the light of 'man's larger understanding of the universe, his scientific achievements, and deeper appreciation of brotherhood' (American Humanist Association, 1933). A cosmopolitan perspective engages both the intellect and the emotions. The concept of idealised family implies a feeling of belonging and pride in being part of the human community in all its diversity and varied histories, cultures and achievements.

Whilst nation-states, since the nineteenth century, have used education, culture and sport to create imagined communities based on nationality, late twentieth-century processes of migration and globalisation challenge the claims of nation-states to provide a primary sense of belonging. The compelling attraction of the UDHR derives from its capacity to provide an alternative account of what binds human beings together, beyond theories of nationalism. Cosmopolitan perspectives do not inevitably negate the emotional ties of nationhood that many people espouse. Instead they encourage us to reconceptualise all communities, including the local and national, as cosmopolitan. Cosmopolitanism challenges perspectives that privilege national solidarities over all others.

Human rights law is founded on a cosmopolitan perspective. All those, including irregular migrants, who reside within the jurisdiction of a state which is signatory to a human rights treaty, are entitled to human rights and protection. Consequently, some of the most high profile legal campaigns in Europe and the USA involve claims for justice for non-nationals, such as those incarcerated by the US government in Guantanamo Bay or by the British government in Belmarsh prison (Nash, 2009).

UDHR as utopian vision

The preamble to the UDHR is essentially a prediction. It claims that universal respect for human rights will constitute 'the foundation of freedom, justice and peace in the world'. This assertion is perhaps the greatest of the 'large and unsubstantiated claims' made in the UDHR (Freeman, 2002:10). This prediction or promise constitutes a utopia, defined as a vision of a good place that is currently no place (Halpin, 2003).

The sociological concept of utopia is used as a means of challenging dominant discourses and justifications for unequal social and economic conditions. A utopia must not be so idealistic as to be near impossible or require massive coercion to achieve. Karl Mannheim in 1930 conceptualised utopia as not 'an unreal portrayal of the future but a giving to the world a meaning which is viewed as a possibility for its future' (quoted in Sargent, 2008:264). Utopia as possibility has been theorised by Giddens as 'utopian realism' (1990:156) and by Rawls as 'realistic utopia' (1999:128). Looking at ideal solutions but relating them to actual social trends and developments may help to address specific social and political problems. Utopian realism is a space where life politics, based on freedom to create a fulfilling life, meets emancipatory politics. Personal fulfilment and human struggle for freedom from inequalities may coincide (Giddens, 1990).

A utopia has been compared poetically to a horizon. As we take steps towards it, it seems to retreat. However, what we see encourages us to go forward (Torres and Teodoro, 2007). Mannheim also saw utopia as a driving force motivating humans to exercise agency and shape history ([1936] 1991). Outcomes are not necessarily positive. Historian Jay Winter distinguishes between 'major utopias' such as the catastrophic and failed totalitarian projects of Nazism and Communism and 'minor utopias' such as the drafting of the UDHR. The UDHR identified a series of steps that might be taken to lead away from war and oppression. This vision does not provide all the answers, instead it supports the human imagination to 'sketch out a world very different from the world we live in, but from which not all social conflict or oppression has been eliminated' (Winter, 2006:3).

Utopia requires and encourages imagination; it is this process of imagining utopia that has the capacity to challenge dominant discourses and taken for granted assumptions. As Paul Ricoeur observed: 'usually we are tempted to say that we cannot live in a way different from the way we presently do. The utopia, though, introduces a sense of doubt that shatters the obvious' (quoted in Sargent, 2008:269).

Education is a potentially emancipatory process that may offer a means to a different and better future, both for individuals and for society. The proposition that schools and education systems require vision and a utopia is not in itself original (Halpin, 2003; Torres and Teodoro, 2007). We propose conceptualising utopia as justice and peace in the world, based on a common understanding of and commitment to human rights and fundamental freedoms. Whilst there is no philosophical possibility of grounding the claim that this utopia has the capacity to address injustice and violence, we can examine the conceptual underpinning of this vision and explore its elements, namely specific human rights. We argue that this vision permits a challenge and critique to the status quo and gives a sense of purpose to education.

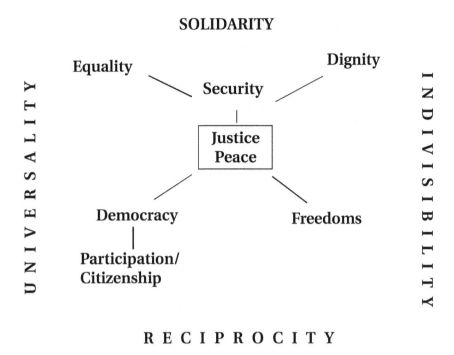

Figure 4.1: Human rights concepts

Human rights concepts

Figure 4.1 presents the cosmopolitan vision of the UDHR diagrammatically, enabling us to see the relationship between the goal of justice and peace in the world, and key human rights concepts. The realisation of justice and peace is at the heart of the human rights project and this is closely linked to issues of security, both personal and global. All human beings are entitled to equal dignity and equality of rights. Human rights can only be fully realised when individuals have an opportunity to participate in decision-making, and this implies democratic practices. Democracy safeguards fundamental freedoms and it depends on these political freedoms for its operation, enabling participation and the exercise of citizenship, without which it cannot be effective.

However, as Freeman (2002) points out, human rights and democracy have independent and potentially competing theoretical foundations. Democracy is a political construct based on the premise that the people should rule. Human rights is a moral and legal concept that provides a set of principles against which the performance of governments can be judged. They therefore limit the power of governments since even democratically elected lawmakers may overturn human rights. Whilst democratic power may be given to elected representatives, human rights theory limits this power and looks to judges and courts to provide checks and balances in the defence of individual freedoms.

The cosmopolitan principle of universality informs all the other concepts: rights belong to all members of the human family. Rights are indivisible; they come as a package, they are not offered as a menu from which individuals or governments can select. This is not to deny that there may often be tensions between competing rights, such as freedom of opinion and expression on the one hand, and the right to a fair and public hearing by an independent tribunal, in the case of a criminal charge, on the other. The freedom of the press is not limitless, and newspapers do not have the right to publish material that might prejudice a fair trial.

Rights demand human solidarity; something that is at the heart of cosmopolitanism. We need to be willing to recognise and defend the rights of strangers, including people with different cultures and belief systems from our own. Finally, there is the key concept of reciprocity. Person A's rights cannot be secured unless Person B is prepared to defend them, and vice versa. This means that inherent in the concept of human rights is the notion of responsibility. We have a responsibility to protect the rights of others.

Four freedoms

The second paragraph of the preamble to the UDHR provides more detail of the human rights vision, namely 'the advent of a world in which human beings shall enjoy freedom of speech and belief and freedom from fear and want'. This is not a vision imposed from above but rather 'the highest aspiration of the common people'.

The four freedoms were first set out in an address by US President Franklin J. Roosevelt to Congress in January 1941: freedom of speech, freedom of belief, freedom from fear, freedom from want. Freedom of speech and belief are sometimes defined as negative freedoms since it is argued that they simply require inaction by government. In fact, upholding them can be costly. Modern liberal democratic nation-states are required to put in place laws, institutions and mechanisms to protect citizens from the abuse of freedom of expression such as hate speech and to ensure that political processes enable minorities to be heard.

The two other freedoms are freedoms from. The first is the psychological freedom from fear. Laws and policing by the state offer security through 'the subjection of power to the reason of law' (Douzinas, 2000:5). Freedom from want is the right of access to basic standards of nutrition, health care, income and shelter. Without these, human beings are deprived of their capacity to develop their capabilities and thus effectively robbed of their dignity and personal liberty (Sen, 1999).

Most of the articles of the UDHR defend and promote freedoms. Thinking of the rights of the UDHR in relation to the freedoms they promote can act as a heuristic device. It is a way of organising the information which may help understandings both of the extent and the limitation of the rights guaranteed in the UDHR. Freedoms are not absolute. The powerful may use unregulated freedom to exploit or oppress. A human rights perspective balances freedoms with a concern for equality of access to rights. Freedoms are exercised in society and claims are constrained by the principle that all other human beings can claim the same right. The rights of the individual may be constrained if a claim is at another's expense.

Freedom of belief

Figure 4.2 presents seven articles that enable freedom of belief and freedom of speech. These articles are mutually supporting. Article 18 states that: 'Everyone has the right to freedom of thought, conscience and religion'. It applies to religious and secular beliefs, including political opinions. It applies to individual beliefs and to those held in common with a religious, philosophical or political community. The right includes freedom to change religion or belief and to practise or manifest these beliefs through 'teaching, practice, worship and observance'. Individuals may manifest their political or religious beliefs by wearing clothes or symbols. The right to change religion or belief means that an individual is not obliged to remain in the particular faith community into which they are born. Freedom of thought, conscience and religion depends on the upholding of a range of other rights, including those

---

12. Respect for privacy

18. Freedom of thought, conscience and religion

19. Freedom of opinion and expression

20. Freedom of peaceful assembly

21. Right to democratic process and participation

26. Right to education and human rights education

27. Right to participate in cultural life and to intellectual property

---

Figure 4.2: Articles of the UDHR enabling freedom of speech and belief

to receive and transmit information, to move freely, to participate in political processes and to have access to education and cultural life.

Freedom of speech

Like freedom of belief, freedom of speech depends on the observance of all other articles in Figure 4.2. It is not an unfettered freedom and is limited by the need to respect the rights and freedoms of others. Freedom of peaceful assembly (Article 20) protects congregations that come together to worship; it equally protects those who wish to participate in or organise political rallies and trade union activities. Individual freedom is the principle, but it is always within a social context. Article 12 protects privacy, that is, the freedom from the intervention of the state in private communications and correspondence and the protection of the law against slander and defamation. Article 19, freedom of opinion and expression, includes a right to disseminate and receive information through any media regardless of frontiers. This requires that states refrain from exercising censorship of the media or blocking access to radio or television broadcasts or internet sites.

The right to participate democratically in government, directly or indirectly (Article 21), is guaranteed. Although there are many ways in which democratic principles can be translated into institutions and processes, the right to a democratic society is a right in itself and, as Article 29 makes clear, is also the context for all other rights. It is notable that the UDHR and the two International Covenants refer only to a 'democratic society' and not to a democratic state. However, Article 21.3 expressly refers to 'the will of the people' as the authority of government and to the right to 'periodic and genuine elections', 'universal and equal suffrage' and 'free voting procedures'.

The vision of freedom, justice and peace within the UDHR implies democratisation in the sense of expanding democratic spaces within and across societies. This applies equally to established and to emerging democratic states, since democracy is a principle as much as a set of institutions. The 1993 World Conference on Human Rights in Vienna proclaimed democracy, development and human rights to be 'interdependent and mutually reinforcing' (UNHCR, 1994:195). Democracy is a dynamic process of enabling people to live together through the provision of security and justice. It is what John Dewey ([1916] 2002:101) referred to as 'more than a form of government: it is primarily a mode of associated living, of conjoint communicated experience'. It is this understanding of democracy that is particularly relevant to schools and education systems.

The right to education (Article 26), is an enabling right. Education supports participation in a range of ways. It provides access to a variety of information that enable individuals to make informed choices and to critically review their political, religious, ideological and traditional beliefs. It includes the right to human rights education and to an understanding of rights. This is important since a right is only an effective right when it is known. The right to participate in cultural life (Article 27) is in a sense an extension of the right to education since it is through an experience and understanding of the arts and sciences that individuals are able to enjoy society's benefits and to express their own human creativity.

No freedoms are absolute, however, and they may be limited under Article 29b by permissible laws that are enacted in order to protect the equal rights of others and meet 'the just requirements of morality, public order and the general welfare in a democratic society'. So, for example, nation-states may restrict freedoms so as to prevent child abuse and to prevent images of child abuse being circulated. In doing so, they are acting to protect human rights.

Freedom from want

Figure 4.3.summarises the articles enabling freedom from want. These are intended to ensure that human beings have sufficient material resources and protection to enable them to access their fundamental human rights. Extreme poverty denies access to life, health, education and participation.

The right to social security (Article 22) is guaranteed to 'everyone, as a member of society' and not just to citizens of the nation-state. States clearly have a responsibility to ensure that all inhabitants have access to adequate resources to enable them to live with dignity and develop as human beings. The other articles in this section amplify this vision of what it means to live in dignity. The right to work (Article 23) is also the right to fair pay and to rest and leisure (Article 24). Article 25 requires the state to ensure to everyone a standard of living adequate for healthy living. Precisely how this is to be achieved is again a site of struggle involving political parties, trades unions and NGOs.

---

22. Right to social security and economic, social and cultural rights

23. Right to work and fair pay

24. Right to rest and leisure

25. Right to adequate healthy standard of living

Figure 4.3: Articles of the UDHR enabling freedom from want

There is a clear understanding that this will involve global solidarity. There is recognition of human interdependence and an implicit acknowledgement that the actions or inactions of one group or nation may well impact on others.

The United Nations characterises access to these 'freedom *from*' (as opposed to 'freedom *to*') rights as development. In this context it is frequently argued that fiscal resources limit the extent to which governments can guarantee rights. In fact the Vienna Declaration of the World Conference on Human Rights is quite specific in asserting that:

> While development facilitates the enjoyment of all human rights, the lack of development may not be invoked to justify the abridgement of internationally recognised human rights (UNHCR, 1994:197).

Responsibility for ensuring access to economic and social rights lies partly with the more powerful economies that have historically exploited terms of trade with those they have subjugated. All governments are required to address issues of corruption and governance.

Freedom from fear

Struggles for freedoms are in fact struggles for self-realisation, fulfilment and creativity. The UDHR is a utopian vision that provides a language to define and justify concerted action for change, promoting solidarity. It is thus an 'open text, whose reference is past conflict and whose performance will help to decide future struggles' (Douzinas, 2000:95).

Freedom from fear is linked closely to freedom of speech and belief. Individuals are entitled to protection from arbitrary and cruel actions by agents of the state, including protection of the right to life. Fear of such abuses threatens political freedom. Individuals and groups should be able to go about their lawful and peaceful business, including participation in political, trades union and cultural activities without fearing unjustified arrest, detention or exile (Article 9). They may own property and this is not subject to confiscation by the state (Article 17). When arrested, there should be a due legal process that recognises the individual as a person before the law (Article 6) who is guaranteed equal treatment by the law (Article 7). Trials should be held in public and be conducted fairly (Article 10). There must be a presumption of innocence unless proven otherwise and no one can be convicted for something that, at the time of the supposed offence, was not illegal (Article 11).

> 3. Right to life
>
> 4. No slavery
>
> 5. No torture
>
> 6. Recognition as a person before the law
>
> 7. Equal protection by law
>
> 9. No arbitrary arrest, detention, exile
>
> 10. Fair, public trial
>
> 11. Presumed innocence and no retroactive laws
>
> 14. Right to asylum
>
> 17. Right to own property
>
> 28. Security – national and international promotion and protection of rights
>
> 29. Duties and no right to undermine UN principles
>
> 30. No government or group may destroy these rights and freedoms

Figure 4.4: Articles of the UDHR enabling freedom from fear

Freedom from fear is also protected by international law and the inter-national human rights regime (Article 28). Articles 29 and 30 assert both limitations to rights and the indivisibility of human rights. Rights and free-doms must not undermine human rights or act counter to the spirit of the UN Charter. Article 28 reminds individuals of their responsibilities to their com-munities. However, it should be noted that: 'A society based on rights does not recognise duties; it acknowledges only responsibilities arising from the reci-procal nature of rights in the form of limits on rights for the protection of the rights of others' (Douzinas, 2000:10). Although Article 28 invokes a sense of duty to the community, duty is undertaken from a sense of moral conviction rather than state coercion.

The UDHR and state oppression

Human rights are part of a struggle for civilisation against barbarity. The second paragraph of the preamble to the UDHR sets out a double case: 'dis-regard and contempt for human rights have resulted in barbarous acts which have outraged the conscience of mankind ...'. The Declaration comes into being because humanity is outraged by inhumanity to fellow humanity. Human rights need to be reasserted so as to protect future generations from barbarity or, in the words of the UDHR, 'disregard and contempt for human rights'. The UDHR asserts moral standards requiring nation-state signatories to recommit themselves and their agents, including the police, the military and the judiciary, to uphold these standards.

Nazi decrees by year	UDHR response
Some 2000 discriminatory decrees were made. The following is a small selection	
1933	
Police and the courts no longer protect Jews from attack	Article 7: All are equal before the law and are entitled without any discrimination to equal protection of the law
Kosher – ritual slaughter of animals – banned	Article 18: Everyone has the right to manifest his religion or belief in teaching, practice, worship and observance
1934	
Jewish students excluded from exams in medicine, dentistry, pharmacy and law	Article 26: Everyone has the right to education
1935-6	
Ban on 'mixed marriages'	Article 16: Men and women of full age, without any limitation due to race, nationality or religion, have the right to marry and to found a family
Jews deprived of German citizenship and right to vote.	Article 15: No one shall be arbitrarily deprived of his nationality.
Benefit payments to large Jewish families stopped.	Article 22: Everyone, as a member of society, has the right to social security
Jews banned from parks, restaurants and swimming pools.	Article 24: Everyone has the right to rest and leisure.
Jews no longer allowed electrical/optical equipment, bicycles, typewriters or records	Article 19: Everyone has the right to seek, receive and impart information and ideas through any media and regardless of frontiers.
1938	
Jews excluded from cinema, theatre, concerts, exhibitions, beaches and holiday resorts	Article 27: Everyone has the right freely to participate in the cultural life of the community
1939	
Jews' radios confiscated	Article 19: as above
Jewish curfew established	Article 13: Everyone has the right to freedom of movement within the borders of each State.

Nazi decrees by year	UDHR response
1940	
Jews' telephones confiscated	Article 19: as above.
1941	
Jews over 6 forced to wear a Yellow Star of David with 'Jew' written on it	Article 2: Everyone is entitled to all the rights and freedoms set forth in this Declaration, without distinction of any kind, such as race, colour, sex, language, religion, political or other opinion, national or social origin, property, birth or other status.
Jews forbidden to use public telephones	Article 19: as above.
Jews forbidden to leave the country	Article 13: Everyone has the right to leave any country, including his own, and to return to his country.
1942	
Jews forced to hand over fur coats and woollen items	Article 17: No one shall be arbitrarily deprived of his property.
All schools closed to Jewish children	Article 26: as above.
1943	
Continuous deportations to death camps	Article 3: Everyone has the right to life, liberty and security of person.
	Article 4: No one shall be held in slavery or servitude.
	Article 5: No one shall be subjected to torture or to cruel, inhuman or degrading treatment or punishment.
	Article 6: Everyone has the right to recognition everywhere as a person before the law.
	Article 7: as above.
	Article 9: No one shall be subjected to arbitrary arrest, detention or exile.

Figure 4.5: The UDHR as a response to Nazi anti-Jewish decrees 1933-43. Based on material © British Library, n/d. (continued)

The UDHR assumes a collective conscience that extends to the whole of humanity, 'the conscience of mankind'. It is conscience that enables human beings to distinguish between right and wrong, civilisation and barbarity. The UDHR proposes the terms on which this conscience can be brought to bear in all contexts. Respect for human rights constitutes the good and abuse of human rights the morally wrong.

Totalitarian regimes adopt alternative moral standpoints. They may invoke utilitarian or scientific positivist perspectives. Utilitarianism uses the greatest good for the greatest number as its standard. This standpoint disregards minorities, forcing them into compliance. Scientific positivism presents science as incontrovertible authority. The regime may claim scientific management of the economy to justify restrictions on freedoms and absolute state control. Science has also been used to justify apartheid, eugenics and social Darwinism. Human rights challenge perspectives that deny the equal right of all individuals to dignity.

The UDHR may be read as a direct reaction to the use of the law by the state in Nazi Germany. Within a month of coming to power in 1933, Hitler revoked the section of the Weimar constitution that guaranteed personal liberty. His decree over-rode former legal safeguards and allowed agents of the state to restrict freedom of expression, freedom of the press, and freedom of assembly and association. Privacy laws were ignored, allowing state agents to intercept postal and telephone communications, search houses and confiscate property. Proclaimed in the immediate aftermath of the Reichstag fire, the decree was seen as a political attack on Communists, and had a measure of popular support. Once in place it was applied and extended to any other so-called enemies of the state. The abolition of the right to personal liberty enabled Nazi militias to detain political enemies without the involvement of the police or the courts (Kershaw, 1995).

The Nazi regime then enacted a succession of decrees targeting Jewish Germans. Figure 4.5 sets out some of the Nazi decrees against German Jews enacted between 1933 and 1943. Against each is an article of the UDHR that appears to have been drafted in response to that particular decree. The UDHR can be read as a direct response to state-enacted barbarity, warning states of legislation of administrative decrees that are inadmissible since they deny justice, peace and human dignity. The UDHR has not put an end to un-just laws, but it provides standards that can be used by groups campaigning for freedoms and social justice.

Conclusion

This chapter has considered the origins of the utopian cosmopolitan vision provided by the UDHR. This vision is grounded in real experience of the inhumane and unjust actions of states and their agents. A perspective informed by the UDHR provides a way of exploring political solutions to global and to educational issues that takes into account issues of power and the distribution of resources. The UDHR has the potential to transform education and schooling. Education systems and institutions including schools require a clear-sighted vision on the part of leadership and one that can be easily conveyed to all stakeholders.

The UDHR presents a cosmopolitan utopian vision. It invites the international community to examine society and the state of the world as it actually is and imagine it as it could be. A critical examination of human rights enables a deeper understanding of political processes and a way of reading the world. Part One of *Teachers and Human Rights Education* has critically examined human rights and the human rights framework as an agenda for action. In Part Two, we examine more closely the strengths and limitations of human rights for realising peace and justice in multicultural societies and in today's unequal and unjust world.

Conclusion

5

Women's human rights

'**W**omen's rights are human rights' has become a powerful and important campaigning slogan for women across the globe in recent decades. From the late 1980s and early 1990s women in many different countries began to work together as part of a global movement, using the human rights framework to develop analytical and political tools that we recognise today as the concepts and practice of women's human rights.

This chapter examines the idea that women's rights are human rights. It argues that full recognition of women's rights as human rights has considerable and complex implications for an understanding of human rights generally. It has implications for all people, regardless of gender. It also has particular implications for teachers, both generally and specifically as human rights educators.

The assertion that that women's rights are human rights appears at first sight to be simple, self-evident, and uncontroversial. No one is likely to refute it by arguing that women are not fully human, or that human rights documents do not apply to women. Yet, used as a campaigning tool it has proved to be transformatory.

The global movement for women's human rights grew out of concerns that in countries across the world women do not enjoy the respect and dignity they deserve as human beings. The Universal Declaration of Human Rights (UDHR) confirmed the twin principles of equal dignity and non-discrimination. It proclaimed 'All human beings are born free and equal in dignity and rights' (Article 1), and stressed the principle of non-discrimination in the enjoyment of these rights:

Everyone is entitled to all the rights and freedoms set forth in this Declaration, without distinction of any kind, such as race, colour, sex, language, religion, political or other opinion, national or social origin, property, birth or other status (UDHR, Article 2).

Despite these ideals, women continue to experience particular barriers in claiming their rights. From 1948, when universal human rights were recognised by the international community, until the early 1990s, human rights instruments, concepts and practices appeared ill-adapted to the particular needs and experiences of women. Women found themselves marginalised and disadvantaged, with inequalities and abuses of their rights going unchecked. As Bunch and Frost (2000) have argued:

This marginalisation of women in the world of human rights has been a reflection of gender inequity in the world at large ... It has contributed to the perpetuation, and indeed the condoning, of women's subordinate status. It has limited the scope of what was seen as governmental responsibility, and thus has made the process of seeking redress for human rights violations disproportionately difficult for women and in many cases outright impossible.

Efforts to realise women's human rights have grown out of women's determination that their full humanity be recognised and that human rights concepts and practices be developed so that women and girls enjoy equal dignity and protection of human rights, alongside men and boys, simply as human beings. The circumstances of women's lives have meant that specific treaties and agreements have been developed to guarantee women's particular interests and concerns, related, for example, to reproductive rights and freedom from violence.

Women's activism and the development of human rights

Human rights, as identified in the UDHR and found in the International Covenant on Civil and Political Rights (ICCPR) and the International Covenant on Economic, Social and Cultural Rights (ICESCR), apply equally to all women and men without discrimination. But realising these rights for women and ensuring equality by including rights which apply specifically to women has involved a campaign which is ongoing.

An initial and important step in realising women's human rights was the Convention on the Elimination of all Forms of Discrimination Against Women (CEDAW) which was adopted by the United Nations in 1979 and came into force in 1981. A Convention is a legally binding instrument and CEDAW was the first such international instrument to prohibit discrimination against women. The governments of all UN member-states which ratify CEDAW are obliged to take affirmative action to advance women's equality and address patterns of discrimination. At the time of writing, 185 countries, which represent over ninety per cent of member-states, have ratified the treaty (UNDAW, 2009). CEDAW defines discrimination as:

> any distinction, exclusion or restriction made on the basis of sex which has the effect or purpose of impairing or nullifying the recognition, enjoyment or exercise by women, irrespective of their marital status, on a basis of equality of men and women, of human rights and fundamental freedoms in the political, economic, social, cultural, civil or any other field (CEDAW, Article 1).

Every four years, governments are obliged to submit a report to the Committee on the Elimination of Discrimination against Women on the progress they have made in implementing CEDAW. Women's advocacy organisations may submit shadow reports, which may challenge, add or challenge the claims in the governmental report. This is a powerful way in which non-governmental organisations (NGOs) can play a role in working towards the greater empowerment of women. In 2000 an optional protocol to CEDAW entered into force. Member-states that ratify this optional protocol recognise the competence of the Committee to receive and consider complaints from individuals or groups within their jurisdiction.

The UN World Conference on Human Rights, held in Vienna in 1993, and the resulting *Programme of Action*, presented an important milestone in human rights development. It declared:

> The human rights of women and the girl-child are an inalienable, integral, and indivisible part of universal human rights. The full and equal participation of women in the political, civil, economic, social and cultural life, at the national, regional and international levels, and the eradication of all forms of discrimination on grounds of sex, are priority objectives of the international community. (UNHRC, 1994:198)

The conference brought together governments and NGOs from around the world, to reaffirm the universality of human rights. Although the initial conference call did not mention women, nor were there any gender specific aspects of human rights included on the proposed agenda, it became the focus for a global campaign which ensured that women's human rights were centrally promoted at both the NGO forum and the governmental meeting (Friedman, 1995). Consequently, human rights violations which have a disproportionate impact on women and girls and which in some cases can literally be a question of life and death, such as abuse within the family; war crimes against women; violations of women's bodily integrity; socio-economic human rights abuses; and political participation and persecution; were all addressed in the Conference's final *Declaration and Programme of Action*, signed by a total of 171 governments.

The Vienna Declaration marked an important step in a process through which official understandings of human rights were extended so as to place women's human rights and the particular ways in which women experience disadvantage and discrimination more centrally on the agenda of the international community. It inspired women to continue the processes of lobbying at subsequent United Nations conferences. Women's achievements include: ensuring that women's reproductive rights are explicitly recognised as human rights at the Cairo conference on population and development (ICPD, 1994); and establishing an agenda and plan for realising women's human rights addressing the girl child, poverty, education, health, violence, armed conflict, the economy, access to political power and decision-making, media and the environment at the fourth world conference on women in Beijing (UNDAW, 1995). Women and their advocates have also ensured that widespread and systematic rape, forced pregnancy, and sexual slavery are recognised as crimes against humanity in the founding statute of the first International Criminal Court in The Hague (UN, 1998) which came into force in 2002.

Principles for women's human rights

Julie Mertus and Nancy Flowers have identified seven principles for women's human rights which are presented in Figure 5.1. Principles 1, 2 and 3, relating to dignity, universality, and non-discrimination have been discussed above. Human rights cannot be universal without human rights for all women, regardless of ethnicity, national status, disability, marital status or sexuality. Principle 3, relating to equality and non-discrimination, might equally be applied to the human rights of another grouping, such as children and young people, people with disabilities, or any minoritised group. Just as violations against women which go unaddressed or unrecognised as human rights abuses collectively diminish women as human beings, so other forms of discrimination against individuals, for example, on the basis of ethnicity, religion or national origin, may serve collectively to diminish the wider group, serving to deny their humanity.

Principle 4, that of indivisibility, and Principle 5, that of interconnectedness, are important concepts in human rights and in women's human rights in

Principle 1: Dignity

The core basis of human rights is the protection and promotion of human dignity.

Principle 2: Universality

Human rights belong to us all. The universal nature of rights does not mean they are experienced in the same manner for all people. Universality means that governments and communities should uphold certain moral and ethical values that cut across all regions of the world.

Principle 3: Equality and non-discrimination

The Universal Declaration of Human Rights (UDHR) and other international human rights documents afford the same rights and responsibilities to all women and men, girls and boys, by virtue of their humanity, regardless of any role or relationship they may have. When violations against women are not recognised as human rights abuses, women are collectively diminished as human beings and denied their inherent personhood.

Principle 4: Indivisibility

Women's rights should be addressed as an indivisible body, including political, social, economic, cultural and collective rights. These cannot be prioritised or divided into 'generations' of rights, some of which should be achieved before others.

Principle 5: Interconnectedness

Human rights concerns appear in all spheres of life – homes, schools, workplace, elections, courts, etc. Violations of human rights in one area may mean loss in another. At the same time, promotion of human rights in one area supports other human rights.

Principle 6: Government responsibility

Human rights are not gifts bestowed at the pleasure of governments. Nor should governments withhold them or apply them to some people but not to others. When governments do so, they must be held accountable.

Principle 7: Personal and corporate responsibility

Governments are not the only perpetrators of human rights violations against women. Corporations and private individuals should also be held accountable; cultural mores and social traditions that subordinate women should be challenged.

Figure 5.1 Seven principles for women's human rights (adapted from Mertus and Flowers, 2008)

particular. Women's human rights need to be addressed as an indivisible body, including political, social, economic, cultural and collective rights. This is because women, who are more likely to encounter discrimination in education and in employment, and to take primary responsibility for the care of children, often do not enjoy the social and economic conditions that make possible the exercise of civil and political rights and participation rights in public life. These rights are all interconnected; realising one right may help secure another. Concrete strategies to address women's human rights therefore need to acknowledge how denial of social and economic rights can act as a barrier to claiming women's political and social rights, so that efforts are targeted appropriately.

Principle 6, that of government responsibility and accountability, is of considerable importance for women's human rights. As Frost and Bunch (2000) have pointed out, the marginalisation of women's human rights and their subordinate status have sometimes limited the scope of government responsibility for upholding women's human rights, particularly if abuses of human rights take place within the context of the family. Governments have a duty to ensure that legal and justice frameworks protect women from domestic violence and other abuses of their rights at the hands of family members. But this does not mean that Principle 7 should be neglected: individuals and corporations should be held to account, when they endanger or abuse women's human rights. Nor are cultural mores or social traditions a justification for denying women their human rights.

These last two principles are of key importance to teachers in schools. In Britain and elsewhere, schools that have introduced human rights education have often stressed the horizontal relationships between people, as the key relationships where human rights principles apply, overlooking the vertical relationships between people and governments. An emphasis on interpersonal relationships may encourage compliance rather than an awareness of the importance of standing up for rights. It overlooks the power structures which operate in schools and wider society. Schools have ignored or underplayed the fact that governments are accountable for upholding the rights of the people, preferring to teach a form of human rights where heavy emphasis is placed on the responsibility of children for upholding each other's rights.

Teachers may also be uncertain whether the rights of the young people in their care should take second place to the social mores of families or to cultural traditions, particularly in relation to the girl child. Teachers and schools have sometimes interpreted the practice of multiculturalism to mean that they should not act to protect the rights of children, usually girls, when they encounter an infringement of a child's rights which is justified by reference to family or wider community values. This is particularly the case where the child in question is from a different cultural or social community from that of the school staff. Principles 6 and 7 need therefore to be given very careful consideration in school contexts. When social mores or cultural traditions are out of keeping with human rights standards, they need to be challenged. If a child is vulnerable to a potential abuse, such as forced marriage or withdrawal from schooling, school authorities need to act to protect the child, in keeping with human rights standards.

Developing alternative visions

Examining the lives of women and girls through a human rights lens allows us to identify and apply a set of principles by which we can imagine alternative futures and work towards the realisation of those futures, through campaigning and political action. As Bunch (2008:xiii) points out, what is useful about a human rights framework is that:

> It provides principles by which to develop alternative visions of women's and girls' lives without suggesting the substance of those visions.

In other words, human rights are not deterministic. In according each person equal human dignity, human rights principles secure for each woman the possibility of autonomy, freedom and choice. These principles do not insist that all conform to a pre-determined cultural norm, but set standards for the lives of all women, against which they can evaluate their own and others' cultures and experiences. This process of evaluation allows women to identify and describe violations of rights and impediments to realising their rights.

They enable all, both women and men, to see that what we understand by culture is in a constant process of change and development. Human rights can be worked out in different cultural contexts, following human rights principles. These principles provide normative standards. They are universal, but they do not imply sameness. Just as we can read the stories of the three young women in chapter one, and identify the violations of rights they experienced and the factors which served to prevent them from claiming their rights, so too can we do that in other contexts. Thus, understood in this way, human rights principles, as applied to women and girls, are universal, but they may be applied and worked out differently in different cultural contexts.

Political power

On the one hand, the body of international instruments and agreements on human rights provide women with a reference point against which they can assess their lives and imagine different futures, acting as an ideal to which society can aspire. On the other, this body of internationally agreed standards can be used as a campaigning or political tool for realising rights. As Bunch (2008:xiii) points out, 'it gives women political leverage and a tenable point of reference'. Governments do not like to be shown to be failing in their commitments to uphold women's human rights.

Women can put pressure on their government to ensure that domestic laws protect women's interests and are brought in line with the international standards to which the government has signed up. For example, Mertus and Flowers (2008:267) cite the example of Morocco, where the Association Démocratique des Femmes du Maroc (ADFM) has, since 1996, coordinated a large number of NGOs in preparing shadow reports to the Committee monitoring the implementation of CEDAW. By conducting field research and documenting cases of human rights violations and discrimination against women, running workshops, and giving press conferences, ADFM is able to hold the government to account, raising awareness within the country and drawing the attention of the international community to the Moroccan government's record on women's human rights. In 2002, a law was passed requiring a 10 per cent quota of women parliamentarians, and raising the number of women in parliament from just two to an Arab-world record of 35 (Mertus and Flowers, 2008:257).

Following pressure from women's organisations and professionals working with girls and young women, the UK government introduced the Forced Marriage (Civil Protection) Act 2007. This law is designed to protect those living in England, Wales and Northern Ireland. The government established a Forced Marriage Unit which aims to support UK nationals who have been forced into marriage overseas; those at risk of being forced into marriage; people worried about friends or relatives; and professionals working with actual or potential victims of forced marriage. The UK government sees some 1,600 reportings of forced marriage a year (FCO, 2009). Southall Black Sisters (SBS), an NGO which works as an advocacy and campaigning organisation, has advised the government, made recommendations to the Home Office, the Foreign and Consular Service, social services, schools and health authorities. SBS resigned from the government working group on forced marriage when the group insisted on offering mediation and reconciliation as options to women in this situation, pointing out that when women turn to the authorities for help, they have already tried such a mechanism, and need protection, rather than be 'reconciled' in a dangerous and potentially violent home.

The ongoing SBS campaign on forced marriage highlights the need for continued work by activists to protect women from violence, even when the necessary laws are in place. SBS express their concern about the reluctance of state agencies to intervene. It appears that some professionals believe it to be racist to speak out. SBS draw on the concept of women's human rights in their appeal:

> We have been campaigning for a widespread acceptance of the view that it is racist not to intervene and that it is the human right of all women to expect and be afforded state protection against violence (SBS, 2009).

Southall Black Sisters are also able to draw directly on the 1993 Vienna Declaration and Programme of Action and on the UN Declaration on the Elimination of Violence Against Women 1993 (UN General Assembly, 1994), which affirms in Article 4 that in cases of conflict between women's human rights and cultural or religious practices, women's human rights take precedence:

> States should condemn violence against women and should not invoke any custom, tradition or religious consideration to avoid their obligations with respect to its elimination.

Bunch and Frost (2000) suggest that engagement in such campaigns has enabled women to acquire the political tools and international networks that grow out of such activism, equipping themselves with the political skills necessary for the twenty-first century.

The public and the private divide

One of the reasons why women's human rights have been neglected is the result of a divide that has often been assumed, particularly by governments, between the private and the public sphere. The issue of forced marriage, highlighted above, is something which occurs in the so-called private sphere of the family. The private sphere of the family is, within this conception, an area where government should not interfere. In many countries, and particularly in the view of conservative politicians, what people do in the private sphere is considered outside the area of government jurisdiction, whereas what happens in the public sphere is seen to be the proper concern of government.

The so-called sanctity of the family has led to many forms of abuse against women (and children), such as domestic violence, imprisonment in the home and sexual assault, being overlooked, even when there are laws against such abuse. Abuse carried out by male family members, in the name of religion, culture or family honour may be overlooked by law enforcement agencies.

This private-public divide has also been applied at the level of international human rights interpretation, so that the practice of human rights has not been gender neutral. The nation-state has a particular interest in interactions between citizens and the state. Yet the concept of citizenship is itself gendered (Arnot and Dillabough, 2000) and entails formal and informal biases and privileges, related to gender, race and socio-economic status. The typical citizen has been assumed to be male. Those citizens, primarily men, who predominate in the public sphere have tended to give weight to those aspects of human rights in which they perceive themselves as most vulnerable. Thus, abuses of civil and political rights such as freedom of expression, freedom of assembly, and protection from arbitrary arrest and detention have been prioritised. Of course, women have also been able to invoke the same human rights protection, but gendered aspects of their experiences, for example, sexual assault in custody, have often been invisible to courts and have gone unchecked by human rights procedures.

During the period of the Cold War the tendency to separate civil and political rights on the one hand, and economic, social and cultural rights on the other, had a negative impact on women's human rights. The former were associated with western nations, while the latter were seen as the priority of the socialist bloc. This division had the effect of adding to the public-private divide, and making access to rights more difficult for women, whose social and economic conditions have often served as a barrier to the exercise of political rights.

This failure to recognise the indivisibility of rights and the ways in which they are interconnected goes a long way in helping us to understand why women's human rights have often taken second place to those of men. The strength of the human rights framework for women lies in its recognition of the interconnectedness of rights. The human rights framework provides a perspective within which we can examine the ways in which privilege and disadvantage operate in a holistic way. Racial, economic and gender privilege do not operate independently but together, as do racial, economic and gender disadvantage. A human rights framework enables an understanding of human experience which acknowledges this intersectionality.

Global solidarity

As we have argued elsewhere (Osler and Starkey, 2005; Osler, 2009a), human rights are essentially a cosmopolitan project, enabling both scholars and activists to make links between their struggles and those of people in distant places, whom they have never met. This is nowhere better illustrated than when addressing women's human rights. As we have seen, women have been able to draw on international human rights standards to effect change in local communities and in their own nations.

A response by the Committee which monitors CEDAW to women's situation in one country is likely to have an impact on women's lives in another, as nations work towards the realisation of women's human rights. Effectively, the struggle for women's human rights has progressed through the process of global solidarity.

A cosmopolitan outlook and cosmopolitan activism also require that we learn to live together with strangers in our own communities and that we make alliances to struggle for human rights at a local level. The ideal of showing solidarity with women in distant lands is undermined if women are not prepared to work with women to realise women's human rights in their own towns, cities and neighbourhoods.

Recognition of the ways in which local and global issues are interconnected is perhaps best illustrated in the case of migrants and their struggles for human rights. The impact of globalisation on women has been mixed. While some women are realising the benefits, these benefits have been unevenly distributed. Some have seen greater economic security; for others there are greater economic disparities.

Such insecurity has a direct impact on migration. While migrant women are often in a stronger position to challenge traditional inequalities, this is not always the case. The British example of forced marriages is an example of the latter situation. Women who lack access to the labour market, and are excluded from full economic participation as a result of restricted education or language skills are especially vulnerable as migrants. Economically vulnerable women are also vulnerable to other forms of exploitation, such as trafficking and forced employment in the sex industry.

Education and women's human rights

This chapter has sought to demonstrate how the practice of human rights is not gender neutral. Teachers have a critical role to play. The realisation of women's human rights depends not just on global solidarity and local action, but on a process of education. The continuing nature of the public-private divide means that many abuses of women's human rights remain hidden and invisible. Change demands that women and men, girls and boys become aware of women's human rights, and that human rights education in schools centrally incorporates women's human rights.

In practice, this means that, just as the practice of women's human rights has 'entailed examining the human rights framework through a gender lens, and describing women's lives through a human rights framework' (Bunch and Frost, 2000), so education programmes need to encourage young people to consider human rights through a gender lens and learn to analyse critically the lives of women through a human rights framework.

A study of women's human rights will support teachers in developing comparative and global aspects of school programmes. The key message continues to be: 'The human rights of women and of the girl-child are an inalienable, integral and indivisible part of universal human rights' (*Vienna Declaration*, 1993).

6

Human rights and global change

This chapter examines the state of the world's people from a human rights perspective. We recall that justice and peace in the world are both the aim and the vision of the UDHR. We identify elements of the challenges facing the world community that need to be addressed if justice is to be achieved. We then examine ways in which a human rights approach can influence development policies and inspire campaigns for global solidarity, highlighting the role of non-governmental organisations (NGOs).

Inequalities in the world

One of the features of globalisation is that many human beings are now easily able to imagine the 'global village' (McLuhan, 1962:31). This village is a divided and grossly unequal community containing large numbers of destitute neighbours living in impoverished conditions alongside others living in extremely rich and privileged households. In his millennium report to the United Nations, the then Secretary-General, Kofi Annan, envisaged this global village as having a population of one thousand:

> Some 150 of the inhabitants live in an affluent area of the village, about 780 in poorer districts. Another 70 or so live in a neighbourhood that is in transition. The average income per person is $6,000 a year, and there are more middle income families than in the past. But just 200 people dispose of 86 per cent of all the wealth, while nearly half of the villagers are eking out an existence on less than $2 per day. (Annan, 2000:14)

Evaluating progress against the millennium development goals (MDGs), Annan (2005) estimated that 20,000 people die from poverty each day and one billion survive on less than one dollar per day. The vast inequalities in the global village mean that for half the world's population 'there is a far higher incidence of infectious diseases and malnutrition, combined with an acute lack of access to safe water, sanitation, healthcare, adequate housing, education and work' (Annan, 2000:14). The poorest global villagers will feel the effects of climate change first and most harshly. The populations of Bangladesh, Egypt and Vietnam are the most threatened by rises in sea levels. Sub-Saharan African countries are already experiencing drought conditions and this is expected to get worse (UNDP, 2008).

The list of basic facilities denied to vast numbers of people equate with a list of economic and social rights from the Universal Declaration of Human Rights (UDHR), particularly those in Articles 25 (food, clothing, housing and medical care), 26 (education) and 23 (work). Historically, debates and political struggles over world development have tended to be framed in economic terms and less often approached as human rights issues. Today, development is being redefined in human rights terms.

Global challenges: development

The United Nations Development Programme (UNDP), the World Bank and numerous other monitoring bodies report annually on the extent of inequalities in the world. Whilst the situation of the poorest people has remained relatively unchanged over decades, the gap between rich and poor has widened. The rich continue to increase their share of the world's wealth. Comparing the income of the richest 20 per cent to that of the poorest 20 per cent, it has been estimated that in 1820 the ratio was 3 to 1, by 1913 this had grown to 11 to 1 and in the latter part of the twentieth century the gap grew from 30 to 1 in 1960, 60 to 1 in 1990 and 74 to 1 in 1997 (Pogge, 2005).

By the early twenty-first century, the ratio for wealth (not the same as income) was 150 to 1 (Tully, 2008). In other words, relatively few people control the majority of the world's assets. Just three families, through their business fortunes, have a combined wealth equalling the annual income of 600 million people in the poorest countries. The richest fifth consume 58 per cent of the world's energy output and so contribute massively to global warming. The richest one per cent has wealth equal to that of the poorest 57 per cent.

Further inequalities exist at national levels. It is likely that the difference in wealth or income between the richest bankers, industrialists or oligarchs in London and those on the minimum wage or benefits is equally dramatic. Some political leaders and the wealthiest individuals in the poorest nations may well figure in the top 1 per cent of the world's rich list. Although there is still much truth in the notion of a rich North and a poorer South, and a corresponding ethical imperative for wealthier and powerful nations to take action, over-generalised analyses may misinform. The task of realising global justice may appear near impossible. A human rights approach can restore a sense of agency and possibility and help establish solidarity between the global North and South.

WHO and UNICEF report that in 2006, only 60 per cent of the world population had access to improved sanitation. Regional inequalities are such that almost 70 per cent of those in sub-Saharan Africa and nearly half the population of Asia have no hygienic system of sewerage or human waste disposal. They are denied basic dignity and young children are particularly affected by the spread of diseases including diarrhoea, hookworm, and trachoma. Inadequate sanitation facilities and poor hygiene impact directly on the learning abilities of millions of school-aged children (WHO and UNICEF, 2006:2).

The obligation on governments to guarantee access to safe drinking water and sanitation is well established under existing international human rights instruments. There have been a number of attempts to define a specific right to water and sanitation with NGOs campaigning to strengthen treaty commitments.

At the Millennium Summit in 2000 the assembled world leaders adopted the Millennium Declaration, committing themselves, amongst other things, to making globalisation work as a positive force for all the world's people. The means to this end was to tackle the very worst effects of extreme poverty and the leaders adopted eight millennium development goals (MDGs) with the intention that they should be achieved by 2015. The goals, as revised in 2007, are summarised in Figure 6.1.

---

1. Eradicate extreme poverty and hunger

2. Achieve universal primary education

3. Promote gender equality and empower women

4. Reduce child mortality

5. Improve maternal health

6. Combat HIV/AIDS, malaria and other diseases

7. Ensure environmental sustainability

8. Develop a global partnership for development

Figure 6.1: Millennium Development Goals

The development goals are best understood as tools for engaging governments, in partnership with NGOs and businesses such as pharmaceutical and water supply companies, to take steps to address issues that are essentially about human rights. The extent to which the private sector should be involved in the delivery of the targets is a topic of virulent debate. At issue is whether transnational companies based in the global North should make profits from delivering to some of the world's poorest people a commodity such as water that is a basic necessity and a human right.

In 2007, the UK NGO, the World Development Movement, at the request of local NGOs, campaigned to stop the British privatised water company, Severn Trent, from bidding for a contract to take over water distribution in Nepal. Under considerable public pressure, Seven Trent, the sole bidder for the contract, pulled out of the bidding process (WDM, 2009). Whilst governments in many countries have failed to extend the distribution of clean water to communities, the issue of principle is aid from European governments being spent on private sector attempts to enlarge their markets.

There is a direct relationship between promoting human rights and the MDGs. The right to life is threatened by extreme poverty and hunger (goal 1), by the lack of sanitation that leads to infant and maternal mortality (goals 4 and 5) and by killer diseases (goal 6). The goals also address a number of other articles of the UDHR such as the right to gender equality (goal 3); the right to a standard of living adequate for health and well-being (goals 1,4,5,6); and the right to free primary education (goal 2). The goals themselves aim at limiting rather than eliminating the extremes of poverty and deprivation of capability. They are based on such generalised statistics that many cases of severe deprivation may not be addressed.

There is now an international consensus, articulated by the UN Secretary-General, that the elimination of extreme poverty is a human rights issue best articulated in terms of the four freedoms of the UDHR preamble: freedom of speech and belief, freedom from fear and want. This 'encapsulates the idea that development, security and human rights go hand in hand' (Annan, 2005: 5). Annan points out that an illiterate young man with AIDS on the brink of starvation, even if entitled to vote, is not free from want. Similarly, a woman in well-paid employment, if she is threatened daily with violence and has no access to democratic processes, is not free from fear. In summary, Annan concludes: 'we will not enjoy development without security, we will not enjoy security without development and we will not enjoy either without respect for human rights' (2005:6).

This framing of development as a human rights issue is expanded in a UN paper setting out principles for a poverty reduction strategy:

> Poverty is not only a matter of income, but also, more fundamentally, a matter of being able to live a life in dignity and enjoy basic human rights and freedoms. It describes a complex of interrelated and mutually reinforcing deprivations, which impact on people's ability to claim and access their civil, cultural, economic, political and social rights. In a fundamental way, therefore, the denial of human rights forms part of the very definition of what it is to be poor (OHCHR, 2006:iii).

This conception of development has been theorised as the capabilities approach. It is based on the work of economist Amartya Sen who argues that development must be more than simply meeting basic needs, since that approach does not fully recognise the essential humanity of the poor who 'also have values and, in particular, cherish their ability to reason, appraise, choose, participate and act' (2009:250). Where human beings struggle with extreme poverty, diseases and limited education, their capacity to make a difference and demonstrate their capabilities is severely constrained. The UN has adopted a definition of capabilities to be achieved that includes, but is not limited to:

> being adequately nourished, avoiding preventable diseases and premature mortality, being adequately sheltered, having basic education, being able to ensure personal security, having equitable access to justice, being able to live in dignity, being able to earn a livelihood and being able to take part in the life of a community (OHCHR, 2006:7).

When applied to contexts of poverty reduction, the UN guidelines distinguish between rights with *constitutive* relevance for poverty and those that have *instrumental* relevance. Rights to food, health and participation may be denied where there is an acute lack of economic resources. In this case, the non-realisation of rights constitutes and defines poverty. However, the fulfilment of some human rights can directly help realise other human rights. For example, realising the right to work can help support the right to food. Some rights are instrumental, enabling others. Education is perhaps the most instrumental of all rights.

A human rights based approach to poverty reduction aims to empower. The main instrument for this is human rights education, introducing the concept of human rights into the strategy. This both enables poor people to demand conditions that will enable them to access their rights and simultaneously obliges governments to take these demands seriously because they have committed to the international human rights regime. Of course, governments have many ways of ignoring such demands (Grugel and Piper, 2009).

The human rights based approach to poverty reduction uses not just socio-economic indicators but other indicators that are derived explicitly from a human rights norm and are intended to enable monitoring of human rights and hold duty-bearers, namely governments and administrations, to account. The approach is based on participation and involves accountability, both of which may help to address corruption. Understandings of the inter-dependence of human rights ensure that civil and political rights are given their due weight, since they are essential for participation.

Global responsibilities of nation-states

Article 28 of the UDHR is the entitlement to an international order in which human rights can be realised. This is the human rights principle that under-pins goals 7 and 8 of the MDGs: ensure environmental sustainability and develop a global partnership for development. Since two fifths of the world's population consume 58 per cent of the world's energy output, climate change may be considered to be a function of the emissions produced by the post-industrialised countries and those industrialising countries that produce the majority of the goods that sustain the life-style of the global North. The ex-traction companies, whether oil or minerals, are mostly owned and managed from the richest nations. In other words, the governments of the richest nations may be said to have an ethical responsibility for the preservation of the global environment.

It is notoriously the case that the policies of global financial institutions, con-trolled by the wealthiest nations, the World Bank and the IMF, have histori-cally imposed economic reforms on countries without consideration of the impact on human rights. There is a very strong case for asserting that the practice of colonialism and neo-colonialism was, and in many respects still is, largely responsible for the economic state of the world (Tully, 2008). Put starkly, and from the perspective of the governments of the global North, wealthy nations should come to realise and admit that:

> This disaster is the responsibility not only of their governments and populations but also ours, in that we continuously impose upon them an unjust social order without working toward reforms that would facilitate the full realisation of human rights. (Pogge, 2005:23)

It is this analysis that mobilises campaigns for global justice identified as human rights struggles. Human rights discourse enables campaigning activists and NGOs in the North and the South to find a common language of struggle. Within this understanding, wealthy governments of the G8 or G20 nations are key duty bearers. They have a responsibility to protect the human rights not only of their own populations but also those in distant places.

Education and development

Education is a right and an MDG. It is instrumental as a means to achieve other MDGs. Education provides understanding of nutrition, sanitation and disease, including HIV AIDS. Education has the potential to promote gender equality. It can help understanding of the environment and of how to pre-serve the world's resources. In developed and developing countries, educa-tion can also promote understanding of global inter-connections and enable students to think in terms of global solidarity, not only as a moral or political perspective, but also as an essential strategy for their common future.

Poverty is still the greatest obstacle to accessing education and, where there is also armed conflict, schools are frequently disrupted. The HIV AIDS pan-demic in sub-Saharan Africa has decimated the teaching force. The mid-term evaluation of progress towards MDGs noted a reduction in the numbers of children without schooling. Nonetheless, the numbers out of school still amounted to 73 million children in 2006, including 38 million in sub-Saharan Africa and 18 million in South Asia. Even when in school, completion rates at primary level are low and only a small minority of sub-Saharan African young people access secondary education (United Nations, 2008). The gender dimension is particularly marked in education since 57 per cent of those out of school were girls. Within this group, girls from ethnic, religious, or caste minorities are doubly disadvantaged and account for approximately 75 per cent of the 55 million girls who remain out of school (Corner, 2008:45). Girls are also particularly subject to violence at school.

The role of education, including human rights education, in promoting development is seen as crucial by the UN and by NGOs such as Oxfam. Edu-cation enables the population to monitor the performance of their govern-ment, including both the extent of good governance and possible corruption. Whilst international commitments and national policies can help to focus government priorities, it is education, Oxfam claims, 'that creates the 'voice' through which rights can be claimed and protected' (Mayo, 2005:153). In other words, education provides learners with the skills and the confidence to challenge governments and seek justice. In fact:

> Education operates as a multiplier, enhancing the enjoyment of all individual rights and freedoms where the right to education is effectively guaranteed, while depriving people of the enjoyment of many rights and freedoms where the right to education is denied or violated (Tomasevski, 2001a:9).

It is for this reason that the right to education is at the heart of global policies for development.

Education can help to extend horizons and provide choices. It contributes to the elimination of poverty and offers access to those capabilities and capacities to make informed choices that are the essence of a dignified life (Sen, 1999). Moreover, this understanding of poverty reveals the extent to which the human rights of children are disproportionately violated (Vizard, 2006). Crude, though undoubtedly important, targets such as those attached to the MDGs mask the complexities of the denial of rights. Gender disparities in education need to be seen in the context of feminised poverty, gendered economic disadvantage, ideologies and violence towards women (Corner, 2008).

Whilst education is a right and a global priority, it can also be a source and a site of conflict and violence, exacerbating rather than addressing divisions. Governments can use the school curriculum to promote negative and hostile views of perceived enemy nations and minorities. In post-conflict situations one of the first actions of humanitarian organisations and new governments is to ensure that textbooks are revised and teachers retrained. Examples from history include the de-Nazification of the German education system from 1945 and the de-Ba'athification of teachers and textbooks in Iraq from 2003.

Textbooks, particularly where they are seen to be officially authorised, can be used to inflame conflicts. There were violent demonstrations in China and Korea in 2005 after it was reported that the Japanese government had approved a new history textbook that minimised the actions of the Japanese army during the occupation of Asian countries in the first half of the twentieth century. An earlier similar case had taken 30 years for Japanese authorities to resolve (Tomasevski, 2001b). Israeli and Palestinian textbooks are both said to include negative representations of the other (Murray, 2008). In fact a review of textbooks from the region found extensive evidence of historical inaccuracies and misrepresentations, stereotyping of neighbouring populations and 'mutual delegitimisation' (Bryan and Vavrus, 2005:195). The same study concluded that in Rwanda before the 1994 genocide, textbooks, the curriculum and the way education was organised 'served to discriminate, dehumanise and enforce ethnic division' (Bryan and Vavrus, 2005:192). Thus, whilst education has the potential to contribute to future peace and hold out promises, it can equally exacerbate conflicts.

Furthermore, schools themselves in all parts of the world may be sites of violence and danger. Student-on-student violence may be ignored or minimised by teachers. In many situations teachers have been known to resort routinely to violence and engage in sexual harassment and rape, particularly of poor or vulnerable female students (Harber, 2004). Other examples of schools and students becoming targets of political violence include the Taliban in Afghanistan targeting girl students and the Maoist insurgency in Nepal attacking schools (Smith and Vaux, 2003).

A UNICEF study identified a number of ways in which education can be used to exacerbate conflict, including: the denial of education through the forced closure of schools; cultural repression of minorities; segregated education that maintains inequality between groups within society; the political manipulation of history and textbooks; the inculcation of attitudes of superiority; gender-based discrimination and practices (Bush and Saltarelli, 2000). In other words, education can be part of the problem as well as part of the solution. However, in spite of the potential of schooling to cause harm or involve danger, education is also a powerful instrument of development and a place of refuge and recovery at times of humanitarian disaster (Sinclair, 2004).

Teachers, parents, teacher unions and researchers all have a part to play in monitoring education policy and practice from a human rights perspective in order to support campaigning groups with evidence, case studies and published accounts (Apple, 2008). An example of such a long term and on-going struggle in the UK is the campaign to draw attention to the high level of exclusions from school of black students (Osler and Hill, 1999; Richardson, 2007). The evaluation of a European-funded project aiming to combat xenophobia and discrimination against minorities concluded that NGOs that engage with young people in dialogue about human rights are an effective complement to political initiatives (van den Anker, 2007).

The UN Rapporteur on the Right to Education noted that the goal of universal primary education has been pursued as much to promote neoliberal economic targets as to achieve human rights. The World Bank has been condemned for encouraging the imposition of school fees in poor countries and UN agencies challenged for accepting the less demanding goal of improving access to education rather than asserting the right to free education (Tomasevski, 2006).

The right to education has to be seen in the context of the actual practice of schooling. The reality in many parts of the world is that children 'may be sitting in a class with over a hundred other children, taught by an overworked

and underpaid teacher, beaten each time they fail to do their sums pro-
perly' (Tomasevski 2001a:43). Research in India suggests that these conditions
may be compounded by teacher absenteeism, teachers giving preference to
their better paid private tuition after school hours and the prevalence of rote
learning and memorisation (Nussbaum, 2006). Such forms of schooling do
not provide education of a quality sufficient to realise such children's right to
education. Consequently, UNESCO and UNICEF have adopted a new standard, the right to *quality* education (Lansdown, 2007). This is an education
with an explicit commitment to human rights.

Global challenges: the environment

Environmental protection was adopted as a fourth pillar of UN priorities at
the 1972 Stockholm Conference on the Human Environment in addition to
the three original pillars of peace, human rights and development. Environmental concerns led, during the 1980s, to the concept of sustainable development, which in many respects embodies all four UN priorities (Vilela and
Corcoran, 2005). Whilst there is no direct reference to the environment in the
UDHR, Article 28, the entitlement to a social and international order in which
the rights and freedoms of the Declaration can be realised, provides clear
grounds for claims to be made for international action on climate change.
There was little awareness in 1948 of the importance for human society of
environmental issues. By 1989, however, the Convention on the Rights of the
Child included a direct reference to the natural environment in Article 29. It
is the right of children to receive an education that encourages them to respect the environment.

Respect for human rights and respect for the environment were initially
parallel agendas in education and in campaigning but these began to con-
verge from the early 1990s when campaigns and movements to address
climate change explicitly included reference to human rights issues. The
demand was for immediate action from governments who were forced to respond to 'the public awareness of risks' (Beck, [1997] 2000:99). However,
climate change, although increasingly a current risk, has been presented
largely as a future risk threatening the rights of coming generations. This perspective relies on inter-generational solidarity to ensure rights and capabilities to human populations in the future.

Risks associated with climate change include drought, desertification, flood-
ing from rises in sea level and severe weather events such as tropical storms.
All of these have a disproportionate effect on poor people. As a UN report
explains:

> Climate shocks affect livelihoods in many ways. They wipe out crops, reduce opportunities for employment, push up food prices and destroy property, confronting people with stark choices. Wealthy households can manage shocks by drawing upon private insurance, using their savings, or trading in some of their assets. They are able to protect their current consumption – 'consumption smoothing' – without running down their productive capacities or eroding their human capabilities. The poor have fewer options (UNDP, 2008:83).

In other words, poor people may have no option but to eat their seed corn or slaughter their livestock and possibly end in total destitution. Such conditions may also include exclusion from education and health care. These are sources of capability deprivation and this includes limitations on the capacity to assert and struggle for human rights. In such cases, human solidarity may be a major line of defence against starvation.

The UNDP report makes the case for climate change as a fundamental issue of human rights. The drafters of the UDHR looked back on the experience of World War II and the 'barbarous acts that have outraged the conscience of mankind'. Climate change requires a vision forward in time to a prospective human catastrophe. To allow this to develop would be, the report argues, a political failure that would also outrage the conscience of mankind. 'It would represent a systematic violation of the world's poor and future generations and a step back from universal values' (UNDP, 2008:4).

Global Civil Society

Pressure for national governments to play a part in a global response to extreme poverty and climate change comes from global civil society. The hundreds of environmental and development NGOs across the world play a considerable role in public education as well as political pressure. They ensure that issues are debated and solutions sought. NGOs require a framework of human rights and social justice for their actions. They depend on freedom of thought, conscience, opinion and expression. They require the right to seek, receive and impart information and ideas through any media and regardless of frontiers (UDHR Article 19).

Many environmental campaigners with a human rights perspective work through Agenda 21. This comprehensive plan of action, involving UN agencies, governments, local authorities and NGOs, was agreed at the Rio Earth Summit of 1992. It has its origins in the Brundtland Report that first introduced the concept of sustainable development. (World Commission on Environment and Development, 1987). The Agenda is wide-ranging, covering issues including poverty, health, housing, the atmosphere, deforestation and toxic waste. Participation, particularly of young people, is considered central to developing and implementing the Agenda. NGOs work across borders to shape the 'consciousness and perceptions of risk' and promote new methods of protection (Glasius, Kaldor and Anheier, 2006:1). Since the risks do not respect national boundaries and can only be understood by adopting a global perspective, campaigns are both global and local.

Make Poverty History (MPH) is an example, from the UK, of a large-scale campaign timed to coincide with a meeting of the G8 in 2005 when the millennium development goals were to be reviewed. It brought together the major international charity NGOs like Oxfam and Save the Children, smaller campaigning organisations like the World Development Movement and a considerable coalition of churches, trade unions and other groups and was paralled by campaigns in other European states and the USA. It used the media intensively, particularly through a series of ten Live8 concerts that were received 'according to the organisers, by three billion people' (Nash, 2009:143). In other words the concerts generated a total audience of almost half the world's population.

The message of MPH was framed in cosmopolitan terms, namely global solidarity, symbolised by white wristbands. However, unlike the Drop the Debt campaign in 2000, this was never linked to a human rights agenda. In fact, in parallel, UNICEF initiated a campaign to Make Child Poverty History that explicitly used human rights and a capabilities approach to make the case for increased aid to benefit children and their education. Unlike a previous campaign against child sex trafficking, this one received little media attention and seems to have had little impact (Grugel and Piper, 2009).

Instead, the predominant sentiments expressed in MPH were largely charitable, in spite of this being a political campaign. The message for the world leaders was effectively that we are happy for you to spend a little more of our taxes on overseas aid. In other words, please give on our behalf and we shall feel good about helping the poor. The campaign themes and the UK government responses were in fact framed in terms of cosmopolitan nationalism (Nash, 2009). The cosmopolitan vision of the world was well represented, but the campaign was constructed as helping citizens to feel a sense of pride in their benevolent country. This perhaps explains the capacity of the campaign to find support in the conservative media and the relatively successful attempts by the Prime Minister and Chancellor to claim to be leading it. However, whilst the campaign did address policy issues beyond the nation, it at no stage focused on potential conflicts of interest between the North and the South, or on the ways in which these might be addressed.

Other successful campaigns have been explicitly framed in terms of human rights. The Global Campaign for Education (GCE) is a partnership of trade unions, NGOs and international development agencies that came together in 1999 for the World Conference on Education, Dakar. The aim of the coalition, that included the influential federation of teachers' unions, Education International, and was able to mobilise grassroots protests in over twenty countries including the UK, Spain, India, Brazil and Tanzania, was to pressurise governments and UN agencies 'to make – and most importantly to implement – commitments on education as a human right' (Mayo, 2005:153). The coalition was determined for the campaign to be as genuinely democratic and accountable as possible, and it achieved this by ensuring that the opinions and concerns of partners in the South, trade unions and NGOs, were central to decision-making.

Following successful intervention in Dakar, GCE found it hard to find a theme that would challenge the comfortable consensus that education is an unequivocal good. Their strategy was to arouse indignation at the numbers of illiterate people in the world, 774 million according to UNESCO. It drew attention to the fact that two thirds of adult illiterates are women and that the right to education and literacy is also an issue of gender equality. This framing was then used to campaign for the implementation of specific targets such as quality education provision and reducing inequities.

Whether campaigners frame actions for global solidarity in terms of human rights is a matter of political judgment. As we have seen, it is by no means certain that such framing attracts support. Educators, however, can encourage a cosmopolitan perspective that recognises and explores the politics of global solidarity, even where this may mean facing up to realities such as potential clashes between national interests. Certainly, the complexities of issues as apparently straightforward as providing quality primary education in the South can provide case studies of policy implementation that can motivate young people in the North and help them understand how social, political and economic questions are related.

7

Values, cultures and human rights

In October 2001, just a few weeks after the September 11 attacks on the United States in which thousands of civilians died, the UNESCO General Conference adopted a Universal Declaration on Cultural Diversity. Although the Declaration had been in preparation well before the attacks, the meeting provided an opportunity for the international community to assert the normalcy and value of cultural pluralism as an essential feature of human communities and 'to reject outright the theory of the inevitable clash of cultures and civilisations' (Matsuura, 2000) that had been proposed by Huntingdon (1996).

The timing was symbolic, since a liberal model of society, based on freedoms, democracy and human rights, which was clearly under attack from Al Qaida, was also, paradoxically, threatened by the actions of the US government and its allies whose response to the attacks on the World Trade Center was to extend and intensify surveillance not simply to radical Islamist groups, but to a much wider number of people. Members of cultural and religious minorities identified as Muslims in a range of Western countries and/or from the Middle East found their rights and freedoms curtailed, and sections of the media felt free to publish racist and Islamophobic tirades. An official discourse blamed Muslim communities, and Muslim women in particular, for their 'separation' from mainstream public life, overlooking problems of social and economic exclusion (Osler, 2009b) expressed in higher than average unemployment rates, and inadequate housing and schooling. Human rights and fundamental freedoms were curtailed in the name of human rights.

Nation-states were able to introduce extensive, anti-terrorist measures including imprisonment without charge and house arrest, partly by promulgating a message of fear, playing on public anxieties and a broader climate of xenophobia and racism. An existent preoccupation of some governments, particularly in Europe, about whether people in multicultural societies are able to live together (Touraine, 2000), was also ironically strengthened by those government's reactions to groups that sought to undermine their democratic ideals. Such governments also questioned whether multicultural policies based on the premise of equality of rights for all should be revised in favour of policies which emphasise commonalities and present cultural and religious diversity as problematic.

Civil wars in former Yugoslavia (1991-1999) and Rwanda (1994), based on assertions of ethno-cultural difference, suggested that an inclusive rather than a separatist model of society was far from a foregone conclusion. Tensions in local communities which, as a result of globalisation and migration, are more visibly diverse at the beginning of the twenty-first century, may leave such communities more open to exploitation by different political factions. Measures introduced to address extremism, but which unhelpfully conflate religious and political identities, threaten to increase tensions in local communities already experiencing disadvantage and poverty. For example, the Prevent Violent Extremism agenda of the UK government served to define people in terms of one specific identity (in this case Islam) and to label them as potential extremists, provoking anger and alienation among those targeted (Osler, 2009a; Akram and Richardson, 2009). In the face of Islamist attacks, those cultural and religious minorities identified as Muslim became particularity vulnerable.

A specific threat to cultural diversity is the essentialised and singular ways in which cultural identity may be ascribed or claimed. This kind of interpretation of cultural difference ignores the reality that all people draw on a range of identities. UNESCO's Director General clarified that: 'each individual must acknowledge not only otherness in all its forms but also the plurality of his or her own identity, within societies that are themselves plural' (Matsuura, 2002).

In culturally diverse societies there are often a number of groups, including recent migrants and indigenous peoples, who are particularly vulnerable to exclusion from mainstream political and cultural life. This in turn may lead to resentment and disengagement from society. Policy responses are therefore commonly framed in terms of social cohesion. Article 2 of the UNESCO Declaration on Cultural Diversity affirms that inclusion and participation are essential for social cohesion. Article 4 frames commitments to cultural diversity as 'inseparable from respect for human dignity'. It stresses the need for governments to guarantee all human rights to minorities and indigenous peoples. It warns against attempts to invoke cultural diversity as a reason for limiting human rights.

This chapter explores some of the implications of cultural diversity for human rights. It illustrates how a human rights discourse can provide individuals and groups with a tool to strengthen their struggles. Human rights are a set of principles for living together in multicultural societies. As a result of globalisation, societies have started to recognise diversity where nationalist ideologies have previously masked differences. We also examine claims that human rights do not have universal application.

The Cold War: human rights as political rhetoric

Critiques of human rights sometimes reflect the still frequently invoked concept of waves of rights (Klug, 2000). During the Cold War period (1950s to 1980s), the world was perceived as divided into three blocs and each bloc had a different conception of human rights (Donnelly, 2007). The first bloc, Western industrialised countries, emphasised civil and political rights, including the right to own property, as providing the best conditions for capitalism. The socialist and communist bloc, on the other hand, emphasised economic and social rights. In fact, in the early twentieth century, the movement for workers' rights split dramatically over whether to fight for economic and cultural rights within a framework of political rights (social democracy) or to abandon civil and political rights in favour of economic and social rights (Marxism-Leninism) (Touraine, [2005] 2007). During the Cold War, the two blocs sought to use human rights rhetoric to condemn each other's hypocrisy and claim moral high ground.

The third bloc, the so-called Third World countries, were said to focus on third wave or solidarity rights, such as the right to development. In fact, the concept of development until the 1980s emphasised economic and social rights. The right to development was asserted outside a framework of political rights. In the post-colonial context, newly independent states often prioritised national sovereignty and economic development over civil and political rights. Powerful Western countries prioritised political stability rather than human rights in Latin America, Africa and parts of Asia and were often complicit in supporting dictatorships.

The post-Cold War consensus on the indivisibility of human rights (civil, political, economic, social and cultural) was confirmed at the 1993 Vienna World Conference on Human Rights (UNHCR, 1994). Nevertheless, on-going disputes about prioritising economic development over political rights persist into the twenty-first century. Demands for access to the full range of human rights may still pose a threat to vested interests whose representatives mobilise other rhetorics including nationalism and cultural relativism.

Nationalism, cosmopolitanism and multicultural states

The emergence of demands for the full range of human rights challenges the classic foundations of the nation-state. Indigenous peoples and minorities struggle both for rights of inclusion in society and the maintenance of their ethnic, cultural and linguistic distinctiveness in the face of a dominant Western consumerist model (Koenig and de Guchteneire, 2007). However, education has had and continues to have a key role in supporting nation-building policies built on a myth of national homogeneity and cultural identity. Textbooks and the curriculum accentuate the cultural forms of the dominant group whilst implicitly and often explicitly suppressing alternative cultural forms or identities.

The imagined community of the nation (Anderson, 1991) has been created in virtually every nation-state by promoting a myth of a monolithic common narrative of national culture based on a national history and mythology; national heroes; national symbols; a national literature; a national education system; a national media; a national military; national sports teams; and in some cases a national religion and language (Kymlicka, 2003b). The school curriculum and citizenship or civic education, in particular, reinforce national myths and traditions and privilege a national perspective over a cosmopolitan worldview (Dewey, [1916] 2002). Research confirms how schools across the globe promote so-called national values (Torney-Purta, Schwille and Amadeo,1999; Osler and Starkey, 2001, 2009; Reid, Gill and Sears, 2010).

Across the world, the classic model of the nation-state is being challenged and gradually transformed as globalisation helps people to recognise that diversity is a feature of all societies and all nations, including those that may appear homogenous. Youth and older people, women and men, religious and secular, develop different cultural modes of expression and consumption, such as play or sport; homemaking; worship; politics; music; and language. However, in the cultural sphere no one person or group can maintain exclusive ownership of a cultural form. In everyday life and experience, systems of symbols, concepts, beliefs, traditions, rules and ways of organising and communicating can be borrowed, adapted, shared and transposed (Figueroa, 2000). It is perhaps particularly notable with music and food, but it is equally the case with cultural forms such as politics, democracy and human rights. Indeed, 'ideas and social practices move no less readily than, say, noodles and gunpowder' (Donnelly, 2003:88). Just as food and technologies migrate and are adapted, so has the concept of human rights spread and been enacted in the laws and constitutions of countries with very different histories and traditions.

A human rights perspective challenges nationalist myths based on exclusivity. For example, a number of European countries have explicitly Christian constitutions and Christian Democrat parties. Where this leads to those from non-Christian religious backgrounds being presented as Other, it denies them dignity and equality in the political sphere. That is not to say that nationalist and cosmopolitan perspectives are necessarily incompatible; both can coexist. However, the tensions between the two perspectives produce sites of struggle. A cosmopolitan nationalist discourse expresses pride in being a nation with a global vision and a global contribution. This is the discourse of overseas aid but may be no more than 'narcissistic sentimentalism' (Nash, 2009:157). A truly cosmopolitan perspective involves looking beyond national interests in trade negotiations. Politically, the power of nationalist feelings expressed through the media is likely to deter leaders from any position that appears to abandon sovereignty.

However, in a globalising world, a human rights and cosmopolitan perspective corresponds more closely to the political realities for increasing numbers of people (Castles, 2004, 2009). National symbols, cultural forms and institutions are constructs whose claims to authority are founded on notions of belonging that often imply cultural superiority and exclusivity. Human rights, by contrast, recognise that individuals, living in society, have multiple and overlapping identities. Where human rights are guaranteed, individuals may freely choose to belong to or leave any group or association.

One feature of globalisation is that individuals, having experience of international migration or taking advantage of increased possibilities for travel or, minimally, having access to media that enable them to share in the experience of global cultural and news events, may have a sense of a world community. This broader sense of connectedness, beyond the nation, has caused governments to reconsider the basis of the formation of the nation-state and in some cases re-define it as multicultural. This is explicitly the case for a number of countries such as Canada, USA and Australia. Nevertheless, attempts at such historic re-definition are often a site of intense and ongoing political struggle, as can be seen in the UK and other European countries.

In Britain, Government ministers initially welcomed the report of a non-governmental commission entitled *The Future of Multi-Ethnic Britain*

(Runnymede Trust, 2000). However, they distanced themselves in the face of adverse press criticism that claimed that the report undermined British values (Runnymede Trust, 2001). The report proposed six principles for the development of multicultural societies: equal moral worth as a democratic value; recognition that people belong to overlapping communities; acknowledgement of the acceptability of different treatment in order to promote equality; commitment to both unity and diversity; human rights and procedural values as a framework for handling deep moral differences; and recognising racism as a barrier to participation and democracy. Although these principles have not been fully embedded in policies, they remain a useful framework for conceptualising the basis of a multicultural society.

Cultural diversity, far from being a threat to social cohesion, can strengthen societies by encouraging new and more inclusive forms of democracy based on common acceptance of human rights as basic minimum standards. This position is that of a report for the Government of Quebec, entitled *Building the Future* (Bouchard and Taylor, 2008) and the UNESCO *World Report Investing in Cultural Diversity and Intercultural Dialogue* (Rivière, 2009). Although approaches to cultural diversity based on human rights appear to have become part of an international consensus (Banks *et al*, 2005), attempts to implement this model often provoke an outcry by vested interests and conservative commentators.

The struggle for a multicultural society is a struggle for democracy, defined not as 'a model to copy from certain States, but a goal to be achieved by all peoples' (Boutros-Ghali, 1993 quoted in Riviere, 2009:239). Viewed in this way, the focus shifts from the integration of minorities to the development of political systems that ensure the representation and recognition of many voices that have traditionally been marginalised. This struggle for cultural rights to participation is essentially a struggle for political rights and one where women are increasingly taking the lead (Touraine, 2007).

In summary, when a nation-state redefines itself as multicultural there are three major consequences. First, the nation is no longer defined as the possession of a single dominant group. Rather it belongs equally to all citizens. Secondly, it follows that attempts to assimilate or exclude members of minority or non-dominant groups are unacceptable policies. All individuals should be able to access state institutions, and to participate as equal citizens, without having to hide or deny their ethno-cultural identities. Finally, there should be formal acknowledgement of historical injustices experienced by minority and non-dominant groups through past policies of assimilation and exclusion together with some symbolic or other offer of redress (Kymlicka, 2003b).

In practical terms, the shift from monocultural to multicultural nation-states needs to be accompanied by institutional and policy reform, notably in education, to ensure that processes, procedures and practices recognise diversity as a strength in a democracy. This will involve the development of alternative and inclusive narratives such as those supported by Black History Month in the USA and the UK. It will almost certainly require challenging deep-seated prejudices against minority or non-dominant groups and institutional racism. Children have the right to an education that prepares them for democracy and diversity as outlined in the Convention on the Rights of the Child, Article 29b and d, and this is likely to require 'teaching children about the reality of historic injustice, and in exploring why earlier ideologies of nationhood were illegitimate' (Kymlicka, 2003b:154). Such an education will support the skills of intercultural citizenship and prepare young people for engaging with each other on the basis of equality and respect.

Religion, human rights and cultural relativism

The process of accommodating to a multicultural society has undermined some old certainties about national values without clearly offering new agreed standards of judgement. Indeed, there are struggles for recognition within multicultural societies that are increasingly framed in terms of religious observance and obligations. Human rights provide a lens through which political and cultural realities can be examined. In the case of religious observance, human rights guarantee freedom of religion. The struggles centre on the extent to which national institutions, including schools, are prepared to accommodate to demands for recognition by minorities. Responses take different forms in different states. For example, in France and Turkey, headscarves for Muslim girls and women are banned in certain public places such as schools and/or universities. In the UK, ways have been found to incorporate the *hijab* into school, police and military uniforms. It would appear that the right to religious observance cannot be defined in absolute terms; nevertheless human rights provide a standard for interpretation in particular social and political contexts.

In multicultural societies, educators and those working in public services look for standards against which they can evaluate claims for differential treatment on the basis of religion and culture. In education, examples of such claims have included demands to withdraw girls from mixed sports and swimming lessons; the refusal of sex education; attempts to introduce creationism into the curriculum; and a request to allow a Sikh boy to wear a *kirpan*, a symbolic dagger, in school. Discussion and adaptation may well be necessary to ensure access to the equal right to quality education. It is not a question of privilege but rather 'engaging in a reasonable adaptation to counteract the rigidity of certain rules or their uniform application regardless of the specific traits of individuals' (Bouchard and Taylor, 2008:68).

Cultural relativism may encourage concession to all such claims on the grounds that institutions founded by a dominant culture should now promote cultural pluralism. From this perspective, no culture has a right to impose its forms on another and all cultures have equal right to respect in the public sphere. However, from a human rights perspective, there must be judgements about the implications of a culture and its practices for the equal human rights of all. As Freeman argues: 'The principle that we should respect all cultures is self-contradictory, because some cultures do not respect all cultures... cultures that endorse the violation of human rights cannot command our respect simply because they are cultures' (2002:109).

Cultural relativism was the main theoretical perspective of Western anthropologists until the 1980s (Preis, 1996). They asserted that all cultures should be studied, analysed and valued by their own norms. The central emphasis of anthropology was on revealing and interpreting unique cultural features of societies. Scientific objectivity and rigour required that value-judgements be avoided. Since it was argued that all cultures have their own rules and their own coherence, human behaviour was explained and justified by reference to physical context and geography; religion; history and traditions; myths and legends. It was argued that universal rights were a cultural construct emanating from a Western liberal perspective and not necessarily relevant or acceptable in other cultural contexts. Scholars argued that there was no possibility of generating any universal framework of standards or values since such a framework would be the product of one cultural tradition and fail to respect other cultures. Any attempt to promote or disseminate such standards would be an unwarranted imposition and they therefore opposed the Universal Declaration of Human Rights (Freeman, 2002; Donnelly, 2003; Talbott, 2005).

From the 1980s, the concept of cultural relativism began to be critiqued within anthropology (Preis, 1996). Cultural relativism assumes cultures to be static rather than dynamic. It tends to essentialise cultures by analysing them as if they were self-sufficient and discrete with rigid boundaries delimiting one culture from another. Images of essentialised cultures have been constantly reproduced. This approach can still be seen today in many school textbooks for foreign language teaching, history and geography. Such texts present often exoticised portrayals of the way of life and culture of people defined as the Other (Starkey, 2005).

Influenced by discourses and theories of globalisation, a new wave of anthropology began to acknowledge cultural complexity and borrowing. Concepts such as hybridity and creolisation, North and South, centre and peripheries were introduced. It was recognised that ideas and cultural forms can be shared, exchanged, interpreted, negotiated and accommodated. Human rights can be analysed and applied in this way. They have gained widespread currency through a process of cultural interaction and exchange yet they are in a constant process of development as they are interpreted, negotiated and accommodated in different cultural settings.

As Freeman (2002) further argues, a culture is in fact mediated through the voice of the people. In order for that democratic voice to find expression, the people require a secure set of rights. When women, children and minorities are largely excluded from public life, the culture will be defined by the dominant group. Too often, the notion of culture masks the exclusive agenda of vested political interests, incompatible with a human rights approach.

Relationalism

Human rights in a multicultural context promote not relativism but what Figueroa calls relationalism, which is 'a basic recognition of difference/ similarity, of the individual as a divided unity and of the community as a togetherness of different individuals, groups and interests' (2000:55). A cultural relativist approach demands that cultures be judged by their own standards, not by any exterior standards. A relationalist approach is based on intercultural dialogue between groups and aims to work out accommodations that respect the dignity and equal rights of all parties.

In a few cases, disputes over claims on the basis of culture are taken to the courts for decision. For example, a Canadian court authorised the wearing of the ceremonial dagger or *kirpan* in school (Bouchard and Taylor, 2008:62). Usually, such issues are resolved pragmatically by accommodation by all sides and at local level. This requires a clear understanding of the full range of human rights and ways in which some solutions may restrict the rights of others and are therefore likely to be inappropriate. Intercultural dialogue for negotiation of cultural demands requires adherence to certain procedural values. These include: 'openness to the Other, reciprocity, mutual respect, the ability to listen, good faith, the ability to reach compromises, and a willingness to rely on discussion to resolve stalemates' (Bouchard and Taylor, 2008: 55). Reasonable adjustments are likely to be acceptable when they are not incompatible with the overall aims and mission of the school; do not require excessive cost; and respect the rights of others. Each of these conditions requires judgement and interpretation of what is reasonable and may well require some sort of mediation.

Questions of power always need to be considered when engaging in processes of making judgements of 'intercultural evaluation' based on human rights (Hall, 2000:49). An examination of why the demands are being made and whose interests are being served will help to identify the political interests at stake. Those from the dominant community wishing to promote cultural pluralism need to be modest. As Touraine notes, the 'power relationship is always recognised by the dominated party; it must be acknowledged by the dominant one, which in this way will distance itself somewhat from the established order (which is favourable to it)' (2007:180).

Contextualising universal human rights

Since human rights have been formally endorsed by all the governments of the world, as evidenced by the virtually unanimous ratification of the CRC and the resounding declaration of the World Conference on Human Rights in 1993, there is a de facto 'international legal universality' (Donnelly, 2007:9). However, the enforcement and implementation of human rights is hugely variable and largely context-specific. In other words, the enjoyment of human rights is far from universal. The struggle for human rights is far more difficult in some contexts than in others. There is little scope for the assertion of human rights in situations of armed conflict. Repressive dictatorships severely restrict political freedoms and many other fundamental human rights. However, even in liberal societies where human rights appear to be enjoyed, some struggles such as the achievement of equal representation of women in politics and employment make little headway. In other words, there is no country that can boast comprehensive implementation of human rights.

Some governments deliberately restrict human rights for political reasons. Recognition of human rights arose as a response to modernity. They are aimed to protect human dignity from threats posed by market economics and bureaucratic state apparatuses. As traditional forms of society are disrupted by urbanisation and industrialisation, systems of mutual support and obligation break down. Traditional and pre-modern societies based on authority and duties have conceptions of human dignity, flourishing and well-being entirely independent of and not always in keeping with human rights. Such societies may have provided a certain security in exchange for acceptance of duties, but such duties tended to involve extremely limited freedoms, notably for women. Traditional institutions and practices derive from concepts of sovereignty and authority based on duties rather than rights. They are 'alternatives to, rather than different formulations of, human rights' (Donnelly, 2003:71).

Across the world, the modern nation-state has developed according to a standard model with a bureaucracy that regulates and to some extent protects citizens. Donnelly argues that human rights have 'functional universality' since they are 'the only proven effective means to ensure human dignity in societies dominated by markets and states' (Donnelly, 2007:289). In other words, there is empirical evidence of human rights being relevant in every conceivable cultural context.

This argument makes irrelevant claims that human rights derive from a particular cultural tradition, namely Western philosophy. Rather, human rights can be claimed in all political struggles focused on achieving justice (Sen, 2009). Although the values implicit in human rights overlap in many respects with those of the major religious and humanistic traditions, they do not derive from them. Rather, people come to human rights through their own philosophical, religious and/or cultural beliefs. They recognise common values and principles for living and apply them to their own contexts and struggles.

One of the main roles of human rights activists is to translate human rights as codified in covenants and declarations into a vernacular, namely, a form that can be understood and used on an everyday basis within specific contexts. Case studies of the implementation of human rights can be found from around the world. Merry describes how:

> An Indo-Fijian lawyer told me, for example, that she had experienced racism and discrimination in Fiji and in New Zealand and only the international human rights system gave her the tools and consciousness to fight back (2006:2).

She goes on to document the struggle of women in the New Territories of Hong Kong. They were denied the right to inherit property under a British colonial law, which was still in place. This practice was justified as an ancient Chinese custom. They finally overturned the legislation, articulating their case in terms of the international human rights language of gender equity and discrimination.

The invocation of custom and tradition as a reason for denying human rights is often spurious. Traditions are often modern interpretations of a perceived cultural form deemed to constitute a source of authority based on continuity with a stable and secure past. Belief in customs and traditions confers power on those who operate them. In fact, so-called traditions may well conceal very contemporary political purposes, often involving the denial of rights. As Halliday argues:

> even if it can be proved that some particular practice or value or legal prescription is indeed 'traditional' in the sense of having been upheld for a long period of time in a particular community, this need not necessarily entail that it is beyond reform, criticism or outright rejection. (1995:239)

Ultimately, a human rights perspective encourages individuals and groups to challenge discriminatory structures.

Human rights and Asian values

Acknowledging East Asian political leaders' critique of human rights, Japanese philosophers, Se and Karatsue set out to examine the relationship between rights and culture. They argue that there needs to be more cross-cultural debate in order to develop human rights theories and schemes, so as to build on the resources of non-Western societies. Furthermore, they suggest that 'people in every culture should be able to find resources for supporting such a theory and to accept the human rights scheme derived from it *without changing their cultural conditions on a large scale*' (2004:269 our emphasis). Recognising diversity and the existence of sub-cultures in Japan, they nevertheless suggest that there is a specific cultural feature of Japanese morality, namely, that it is situation-based. They suggest therefore that the human rights claim of equal recognition of human rights to all people, justified by a strong tradition in Western political theory which assumes a transcendent moral principle, needs to be explained differently in a Japanese cultural context. They justify equal recognition of human rights by reference to the potential benefits or interests an individual would receive from others. Similarly, they are committed to the human rights concept of freedom of thought, but justify with reference to Japanese culture.

In order to reconcile different traditions and their common acceptance of human rights, but on different philosophical grounds, we might draw on the observation of Appiah (2006:67) that: 'we can agree about *what* to do even when we don't agree *why*'. The human rights project is subject to ongoing development and interpretation; efforts at cross-cultural dialogue which allow individuals or groups to realise a struggle for justice are likely to strengthen human rights.

Se and Karatsue's second concern, that it is important for people from each culture to find specific cultural resources to support human rights theory 'without changing cultural conditions on a large scale' raises a different set of questions, since it seems to assume a static view of culture, something we would challenge. Questioning of human rights is often linked to vested interests and traditional positioning, and is sometimes linked to a reluctance to uphold women's human rights. A further difficulty with Se and Karatsue's discussion is that it takes place outside political contexts, and does not explore the reasons why some East Asian political leaders have critiqued human rights.

Following Singapore's declaration of independence from the British in 1963 and its separation from Malaysia in 1965, its education system was used to forge a national identity based on a rejection of the so-called Western value of individualism, identified with selfishness, and the promotion of morality based on contrasting 'Asian values'. The school curriculum largely ignored human rights on the grounds that such Western values encouraged decadence (Tan, 1994). The discourse of Asian values circulated widely in Asia and beyond and much credence has been given to the claim that they derive from Confucianism. This in turn has given rise to a stereotype of Chinese learners as dutiful and unquestioning (Mak, 2008).

The arguments that Asian values are incompatible with human rights have been very persuasive, to the extent that leading proponents of human rights have felt obliged to challenge this perspective (Freeman, 2002; Donnelly, 2003; Talbott, 2005). Empirically, governments of all Asian states have joined the international human rights regime and now have at least a discourse of accepting the importance of human rights. Yet, conservative forces in a range of nation-states persist in promoting the concept of Asian values, in line with their own political interests.

At a formal level, ministers of the Association of Southeast Asian Nations (ASEAN), meeting in Singapore in 1993, declared their 'commitment to human rights and fundamental freedoms' and decided to 'coordinate a common approach to the application, promotion and protection of human rights' (Manokha, 2009:444).

A number of economically significant Asian countries including Japan, South Korea and the Philippines have systems of government that guarantee a full range of human rights and others, including the Islamic states of Indonesia and Malaysia, have multi-party democracies. China participated actively in the World Conference on Human Rights in Vienna, 1993, and was a signatory to the Declaration and Programme of Action. As a Chinese comparative education specialist explained at the time:

> Along with a reassessment of cultural traditions and Western values, a more balanced understanding has been reached by the young generation and the citizenry of the dialectic interrelations of collective and individual rights ... Rights are a historical concept that evolves along with societal changes. (Zhou, 1994: 86)

This was echoed at the World Conference by UN Secretary-General, Boutros Boutros-Ghali, who asserted:

> To be sure, human rights are a product of history. As such they evolve in accordance with history, should evolve simultaneously with history and should give the various peoples and nations a reflection of themselves they recognise as their own. Yet, the fact that human rights keep pace with history should not change what constitutes their very essence, namely their universality! (UNHCR, 1994:7)

In 2004, the Chinese government adopted an amendment to the 1982 Constitution recognising that 'the state respects and safeguards human rights'. A state commitment to human rights, albeit rhetorical, provides activists with a resource to use in struggles for human rights. There is now also a growing academic interest in human rights within a number of Chinese universities (Weatherley, 2008).

Implications of a global discourse of human rights

A human rights discourse provides individuals and groups everywhere with a common language with which to articulate their struggles. Indeed, so versatile is this discourse that NGOs have applied it to the activities of major corporations. Campaigns for fair wages, decent working conditions and an end to child labour have targeted universally known brands, with some successes. Even the main regulatory mechanisms of global capitalism, the IMF and the World Bank, have adopted policies to promote good governance and human rights. Indeed, it has been argued that the global consensus on human rights is such that they have become the key element of what Foucault called 'governmentality' (Burchell, Gordon and Miller, 1991). In other words, states and corporations 'proclaim their adherence to human rights norms and adopt policies of their promotion without any coercion' (Manokha, 2009: 431).

Some claim that a focus on individual human rights underpins national poli-cies of competitiveness. This has weakened trade union resistance to the im-pact of global capitalism such as the relocation of industrial plant towards cheaper labour sources. Struggles based on freedoms, justice and peace may be tightly constrained by the realities of global capitalism. The utopia may in fact be illusory and merely serve to perpetuate a hugely unjust *status quo*. As Tully wryly observes:

> 'Commerce' or 'economic liberalisation' (a synonym for modern globalisation), by rendering every person and society economically interdependent and com-petitive within an imposed structure of law, pacifies, refines, polishes, makes predictable, and thus – in tandem with representative government – leads humanity to perpetual peace. (2008:18)

Given the vast amount of human misery, suffering and exploitation still pre-valent across the world in the twenty-first century, the argument that the dis-course of human rights has actually contributed to creating or at least per-petuating global injustice deserves consideration. However, any solution to injustice and suffering in the world also lies in struggle. Human rights dis-course powerfully frames struggles for human dignity wherever they occur. Human rights provide a sense of agency and allow for global solidarities. They do not sanction fatalism in the face of global capitalism; rather they inspire myriads of interruptive interventions.

Part 3
Human rights and democracy in schools

8
Children's human rights

In this third and final part of *Teachers and Human Rights Education*, we examine human rights and democracy in schools. The UN Convention on the Rights of the Child (CRC) places an obligation on governments who have ratified the Convention 'to make the principles and provisions of the Convention widely known, by appropriate and active means, to adults and children alike' (Article 42). Effectively, the CRC, which came into being in 1989 and which is the most widely ratified human rights treaty, outlines a set of minimum standards for guaranteeing children's human rights globally. It has particular implications for education policy and legal frameworks as well as for the professional practice of teachers.

The agenda of children's human rights is broad, encompassing children's civil and political rights, as well as their economic, social and cultural rights. As observed in earlier chapters (notably in Part Two of this book) these two agendas are intertwined; those who lack basic economic and social necessities are ill-placed to claim their political rights, and those who lack basic political freedoms will find it difficult to assert their economic and social rights.

In this chapter, we focus on children's human rights in the context of schooling. In doing so, we extend our discussion beyond schools, for a number of reasons. First, the concepts and practice of children's human rights extend to all aspects of children's lives. Children's human rights have implications for educational and other social policy-making and planning at all levels, not just for teachers. In working to implement children's rights in schools, both children and young people and the adults who work with them need to be cognisant of the full range of children's human rights. Secondly, the degree to which children and young people are able to exercise their rights in the wider society is likely to have a considerable impact on the ways they experience schooling, and on the ways they experience human rights and democracy in schools.

Thirdly, the broader study of human rights struggles, including struggles for child rights, need to be part of the school curriculum. Children and young people, working to claim their rights, need to understand the processes by which other struggles for justice, since the mid-twentieth century, have drawn on human rights discourse and law, to achieve support and solidarity. In other words, a critical aspect of children's human rights education, like that of adults, is in enabling children and young people to understand human rights as an agenda for action. This has implications for the whole curriculum, but particularly for pedagogy and content in areas such as history and social studies.

Finally, as we shall see, the right to human rights education, as outlined in the Universal Declaration of Human Rights (Article 26) and developed in the CRC (Article 29) and other human rights treaties, implies that both children and teachers are familiar with the wide-ranging implications of children's human rights and their application for all aspects of children's and young people's lives. This requires that there is education in children's human rights for children and adults alike. Teachers, in particular, require education in children's human rights as an essential element of their professional studies.

All rights are inter-related and the CRC needs to be understood as a whole. There are a number of rights guaranteed by the CRC, which have a direct impact on the right to education, as well as implications for education policy and legal frameworks. These rights are outlined in Figure 8.1.

The CRC cannot be understood as a stand-alone document. Other human rights treaties, including, for example, the Convention on the Elimination of all Forms of Discrimination Against Women (CEDAW), have implications for the lives and education of particular children, in this case, the girl-child; these implications need to be understood by teachers. The CRC has begun to have an impact in legal judgements at international level. Regional human rights bodies have used the CRC as a reference point and interpretative tool. So, for example, when ruling on the European Convention on Human Rights as it applies to the rights of young people under the age of 18 years, the European Court of Human Rights has drawn on provisions within the CRC.

The right to a name and nationality (Article 7)

The right to express views on matters of concern and for these views to be given due weight in decision-making (Article 12)

Freedom of expression (Article 13)

Freedom of thought, conscience and religion (Article 14)

Freedom of association and peaceful assembly (Article 15)

The right to privacy (Article 16)

The right of access to information (Article 17)

Protection from violence, injury and abuse (Article19)

Education and other rights of children with disabilities (Article 23)

Rights of children from ethnic, religious or linguistic minorities or of indigenous origin to enjoy their own culture, practice their religion, or use their language (Article 30)

The right to rest and leisure (Article 31)

The right to protection from exploitative work (Article 32)

Figure 8.1: CRC Articles which impact directly on the right to education

Changing conceptions of childhood

During the twentieth century, conceptions of childhood have been in a state of flux and development. In Europe until the nineteenth century, children were generally not perceived as a different category from adults and tended to be regarded as the property of their parents, to whom they were expected to fulfil particular duties, often playing a key economic role in family life (Osler and Starkey, 1996; 2005). As a result of industrialisation and urbanisation, children's work no longer remained in what was seen as the private domain of the family, and legal safeguards were gradually introduced to protect the children of the urban poor. As Hart (1991) has observed, children's labour was seen as a social fact, rather than a social problem; laws introduced to protect children were arguably introduced not simply to protect children but to protect society from the destabilising effects of antisocial behaviour, itself an outcome of children's abuse and mistreatment.

The international NGO, Save the Children International Union, was active in the 1920s in campaigning for children's rights. The codification of child rights by the NGO received international recognition in 1924, when the League of Nations endorsed the Geneva Declaration of the Rights of the Child, a statement of general principles for child welfare and protection. The Declaration, which was revised and expanded in 1948, formed the basis of the 1959 UN Declaration on the Rights of the Child, the precursor to the CRC.

During the 1960s and 1970s, debates about childhood reflected rapid and widespread changes in societal attitudes taking place in North America and Europe. This period saw a further and significant move away from the traditional view of children as the property of their parents. At this stage, the views of child rights activists were divided between those who argued for children to be accorded the same rights as adults, and those who raised questions about the limits to the possibility of children's autonomy, in relation to adults, including parents and teachers (Archard, 1993).

From this period, mainstream human rights discourse was increasingly applied to children, with the focus shifting from an exclusive focus on the protection of children as vulnerable subjects towards recognition of child self-determination and participation. As Freeman (1992:3) observed: 'The liberationist movement challenged those who claimed the status of children could be advanced exclusively by conferring on children increased protection. The emphasis shifted from protection to autonomy, from nurturance to self-determination, from welfare to justice'. It was in this changing climate that international deliberations began in 1979, leading to the adoption of the Convention on the Rights of the Child 1989. Effectively, the debate about children's political rights was opened.

Today, the CRC is often characterised as encompassing three types of rights: provision, protection, and participation. Save the Children UK have an alternative way of classifying children's rights, suggesting that the rights enshrined in the CRC fall into four broad categories, namely, the right to survive; the right to be safe; the right to belong; and the right to develop. However rights are categorised, the rights enshrined in the CRC are indivisible and serve to reinforce each other.

Article 12 and children's participation

Participation rights in the CRC are to be found in Articles 12-17. Article 12, which relates to the child's right to have his or her views given due weight in matters affecting the child, is complemented by other related participation rights, enshrined in Articles 13-17. Participation rights, which are among those of greatest significance in accessing quality education, are also among those which both governments and schools have most regularly failed to secure. The Committee on the Rights of the Child, which monitors nation-states' implementation of the CRC, has encountered particular difficulties in the area of participation rights.

1. States Parties shall assure to the child who is capable of forming his or her own views the right to express those views freely in all matters affecting the child, the views of the child being given due weight in accordance with the age and maturity of the child.

2. For this purpose, the child shall in particular be provided the opportunity to be heard in any judicial and administrative proceedings affecting the child, either directly, or through a representative or an appropriate body, in a manner consistent with the procedural rules of national law.

Figure 8.2: CRC Article 12

Effectively, the implementation of Article 12, relating to the child's right for his or her views to be given due weight, respect and consideration 'implies a cultural shift in the ways we understand childhood and in the social positioning of children' (Osler, 2010:17). It requires a fundamental review of the ways in which schools are organised, so as to enable and support children's participation in decision-making processes.

The concept of what is increasingly referred to as student voice (or pupil voice) does not adequately conceptualise Article 12 of the CRC. Lundy (2007) argues that current conceptions of pupil voice in education have the potential to diminish the impact of Article 12, since the concept of pupil voice underplays the obligation on schools and education authorities under Article 12. She proposes a model for conceptualising Article 12 which, as well as voice, encompasses space, audience and influence.

Pupil voice refers to children's expressions of their opinions in school, and these may be made directly, or through a representative body, such as a student council. Although Article 12 refers to the obligation on nation-states to 'assure to the child who is capable of forming his or her own views the right to express those views freely in all matters affecting the child' and for these views to be given 'due weight', in many contexts pupil voice merely means allowing children to have a say, rather than to 'assure' their right to express an opinion, a word which, as Lundy (2007) points out, is a strong one, and which implies putting in place mechanisms by which this will happen.

In order for young people to claim their right to express a view on matters which may affect them at school, teachers and school principals need to provide a space or opportunity for them to do so. Student councils go some way towards meeting this, if they are genuinely representative, although many young people are sceptical about the representational nature of their school council, sometimes seeing school council members as an elite group, but arguing that there is little real opportunity for students to become fully involved in decision-making (Osler, 2010). Even when student councils are effective and representative, there also need to be other structured opportunities and legal frameworks for all children to participate in decision-making processes, which may affect them, individually and/or collectively.

Audience implies that adults are ready and trained to listen to young people. Mechanisms for listening to children are unlikely to be effective, unless there is a shift in relationships between teachers and other adults on the one hand and children on the other, in which young people are seen as rights-holders, whose opinions are valued and who are assumed to be speaking in good faith.

Influence relates to the concept of 'due weight' in Article 12. Children need to know that their opinions will not only be noted, but that they will have an influence on the outcome of the process. Influence implies that procedures will be in place so that students can see how their opinions are considered and the impact they have on decision-making. In other words, the decision-making framework needs to be transparent to all, including students. The implementation of Article 12 needs to incorporate the overriding principles of non-discrimination (Article 2), best interests (Article 3), the child's evolving capabilities/right to guidance from adults (Article 5), and also the right to be safe (Article 19).

It is clear that policy-makers in the UK have failed fully to grasp the implications of the CRC, particularly in relation to children's participation rights and those enshrined in Article 12, which require that children's perspectives be taken seriously in schooling. The UN child rights monitoring body, the Committee on the Rights of the Child, documented its concern that in the UK 'there is no systematic awareness raising of the Convention and that the level of knowledge about it among children, parents or professionals working with children is low', noting that 'the Committee regrets that the Convention is not part of the curriculum in schools' (Committee on the Rights of the Child, 2008:5).

The Committee called for the greater involvement of children in policy development, recommending that the UK 'encourage the active and systematic involvement of civil society, including NGOs and associations of children, in the promotion and implementation of children's rights, including, *inter alia*, their participation in the planning stage of policies'. Referring to the principle of non-discrimination, the Committee expressed concern about 'negative public attitudes towards children, especially adolescents', which exist in the UK and which 'may be often the underlying cause of further infringements of their rights' (2008:6).

Additionally, the Committee on the Rights of the Child expressed concern about alternative provision for Traveller children, Roma children, children with disabilities, asylum-seekers, dropouts, other non-attendees and teenage mothers, concluding:

> participation of children in all aspects of schooling is inadequate, since children have very few consultation rights, in particular they have no right to appeal their Exclusion or to appeal the decisions of a special educational needs tribunal; the right to complain regarding educational provisions is restricted to parents, which represents a problem especially for looked after children. [Additionally,] bullying is a serious and widespread problem, which may hinder children's attendance of school. (Committee on the Rights of the Child, 2008:15)

In making these observations the Committee made a direct link between discriminatory practices, non attendance and underachievement of specific groups of children in UK schools, recommending that the UK 'strengthen children's participation in all matters of school, classroom and learning which affect them'. What is clear is that, as Lundy (2007) asserts, voice alone is an inadequate concept for fully realising children's participation rights in education. Professional and academic discourse about *giving* children voice (Fielding, 2004; Rudduck and Flutter, 2004) implies that children do not have a *right* to express an opinion or engage in participative process; instead it suggest a somewhat patronising approach in which adults generously listen to children, but do not necessarily respond to their concerns. An uninformed approach to student voice is unlikely to be helpful in furthering children's rights in schools.

Multiculturalism and schooling

Article 29 of the CRC specifies children's rights within education, outlining the right of the child both to an education in human rights and to intercultural education. Article 29.1 (Figure 8.3) sets out the aims of education for all children. Article 29 refers to the obligation by the nation-state which has ratified the CRC to promote education for peaceful coexistence with others in the community, the nation, and the wider world.

Article 29, 1b refers to the right to human rights education. Minimally, it implies that both teachers and young people are familiar with human rights and with the principles enshrined in the Charter of the United Nations. Clauses 1c

1. States Parties agree that the education of the child shall be directed to:

(a) The development of the child's personality, talents and mental and physical abilities to their fullest potential.

(b) The development of respect for human rights and fundamental freedoms and for the principles enshrined in the Charter of the United Nations.

(c) The development of respect for the child's parents, his or her own cultural identity, language and values, for the national values of the country in which the child is living, the country from which he or she may originate, and for civilizations different from his or her own.

(d) The preparation of the child for responsible life in a free society, in the spirit of understanding, peace, tolerance, equality of sexes, and friendship among all peoples, ethnic, national and religious groups and persons of indigenous origin.

(e) The development of respect for the natural environment.

Figure 8.3: CRC Article 29.1: aims of education

and 1d imply that all young people in multicultural nation-states have some level of engagement and integration with children and young people from backgrounds different from their own, as well as an education which builds on and respects the child's home culture and his or her own identities. Additionally, Article 30 (Figure 8.4), which refers to the rights of children from ethnic, religious or linguistic minorities or of indigenous origin to enjoy their culture, practice their religion, and use their language, has direct implications for schools.

In the UK, the Committee on the Rights of the Child has repeatedly challenged 'the problem [of] segregation [which] is still present in Northern Ireland' where the majority of children continue to attend a school run by either the Catholic or the Protestant churches and where further segregation takes place through ongoing 'academic selection at the age of 11' (Committee on the Rights of the Child, 2008:15). Without some degree of educational integra-

In those States in which ethnic, religious or linguistic minorities or persons of indigenous origin exist, a child belonging to such a minority or who is indigenous shall not be denied the right, in community with other members of his or her group, to enjoy his or her own culture, to profess and practise his or her own religion, or to use his or her own language.

Figure 8.4: CRC Article 30: cultural rights and religious freedoms of children from minorities

tion, it is difficult to see how education can effectively foster respect for 'civilizations different from his or her own' or 'friendship among all peoples, ethnic, national and religious groups', particularly if people from these other civilizations, ethnic, national or religious groups are living in the same city or neighbourhood.

Entitlements to human rights and intercultural education have particular and significant implications for education policy in post-conflict societies, where education systems may continue to emphasise difference, at the expense of equality, rather than promote 'friendship among all peoples'. Additionally, the curriculum may, in some post-conflict societies, emphasise an exclusive national identity which is reinforced through separation of children of different ethnic, cultural and religious backgrounds. Recent or historical conflicts may be magnified or exacerbated by educational arrangements which separate children by ethnicity or religion.

Grover (2007:60) argues that education for tolerance, in keeping with the provisions of Article 29, cannot be fostered where there is complete educational segregation. She concludes that it should 'be acknowledged that educating for peace will require states to mandate some level of educational integration of school children from diverse ethnic, religious, cultural and language groups'.

In England, the government has, since the late 1990s, enhanced the role of religious bodies in providing education. Consequently, the number of faith-based publicly-funded secondary schools has increased, and in some of these faith schools, including those with foundation status, there is less transparency or democratic control over the ways in which religious education is provided than is the case in other publicly-funded schools. Additionally, where faith organisations have control over selection processes, there is a real danger that in some areas, children may be educated separately, according to religion, ethnicity and social class. Research suggests that the admissions procedures of some church schools (which in many cases have been less than transparent) further separate young people, with a tendency in some areas for such schools to indirectly exclude the most disadvantaged young people (West and Allen, 2008).

The challenge of providing education which genuinely educates for living together and fulfils legal requirements to promote race equality under the Race Relations [Amendment] Act, 2000 and community cohesion under the Education and Inspections Act 2006 exists for all schools in England. However, those faith schools which separate children according to religious background face a greater challenge in this respect (Osler, 2007; Berkeley, 2008).

Article 29 makes explicit not simply the right to an education for tolerance and for diversity but the right of the child to an education which also supports his or her own cultural heritage and that of the family's country of origin, as well as the culture and values of the country in which he or she is now living. This right is also implied in Article 30. This raises a potential tension between education for unity or social cohesion within the nation-state, and education for diversity (Banks *et al*, 2005). In times of crisis, and faced with the threat of terrorism, governments may begin to question the normalcy of cultural pluralism, causing them to emphasise commonality over difference. When such policies are applied to education, they risk denial of young people's right to education for living together, enshrined in the CRC.

The importance and inter-relatedness of clauses 1b, c and d are fundamental in multicultural societies and nation-states, as part of the central mission of human rights, and human rights education, to promote justice and peace in the world. They have a particular significance where there are significant power differentials and inequalities, such as the inequalities and injustices (current and historical) experienced by indigenous peoples or which have developed out of a particular history, such as that of slavery and colonial oppression.

Drawing on research into national education policy, we note how a number of different European countries have responded to the imperative within the CRC to promote intercultural education. Looking specifically at the citizenship curriculum, we observe that in neither England nor France does the programme of study give significant weight to the perspectives or experiences of minorities. The French programme roundly condemns racism but fails to explore it. The English programme considers a range of ethnic groups and expects understanding of diversity. It expects individuals to challenge prejudice and discrimination, but does not consider collective responses or acknowledge the existence of institutional racism or structural disadvantage. There is little evidence that in either context minority groups have participated in the formulation of the curriculum (Osler and Starkey, 2009). Until national curricula and discourses about the nation and its history are responsive to minority as well as majority perspectives, it is likely they will remain exclusive (Osler, 2009a) and thus fail to fulfil the requirements placed on nation-states under the CRC to educate for tolerance and mutual respect.

Children's rights, development and schooling
Education is a key instrumental right, which enables access to and supports claims to other social and political rights, including health, social and physi-

cal security, and to participation in cultural and political life. While governments are agreed on the importance of education, making universal access to quality primary education one of the eight millennium development goals, it has proved more difficult to reach a consensus on what constitutes a quality education.

In fact, it can be argued that Article 29, by articulating the aims of education, spells out an agreed position by the international community on what constitutes a quality education. As well as an education which enables basic standards of literacy, numeracy, and economic participation, every young person is entitled to be taught respect for fundamental rights and freedoms; cultural, religious and linguistic diversity and 'civilizations different from his or her own'.

The CRC, in defining these agreed aims in Article 29, which are ratified by all 196 member-states of the United Nations, with the exception at the time of writing of Somalia and the USA, lays before us a minimum standard which all nation-states need to strive to meet. These are not negotiable standards or standards which can be met once universal primary education has been achieved. They are the basic standards to which all nations have committed themselves and against which their realisation of children's human rights in education can be assessed. They imply human rights education which enables young people to participate in the present and to prepare for their future participation in society. Human rights education cannot then be a means of teaching social compliance. Rights-respecting schools must be schools in which young people are taught to expect their rights to be upheld by the nation-state and its agencies, as well as by each other.

9

Citizenship education and human rights

This chapter examines human rights education (HRE) as a right for all, and considers some of the reasons why this right is yet to be fully realised, several decades after the Universal Declaration of Human Rights 1948 (UDHR) was adopted by the General Assembly of the United Nations. The governments of a number of nation-states in Europe suggest that they can fulfil their international commitments to HRE through the teaching of citizenship in schools. Yet a review of citizenship education programmes of study reveals that education for democratic citizenship is usually education for national citizenship.

We argue for an alternative vision of citizenship education, namely education for cosmopolitan citizenship. The human rights project is a cosmopolitan one and effective education for our global age requires a cosmopolitan vision, based on a shared understanding of human rights and an exploration of citizenship at all levels, from the local, encompassing the national, but extending to the global. We consider some of the challenges in implementing HRE in schools in a range of national contexts and consider the strengths and limitations of education for democratic citizenship (EDC) as a vehicle for teaching and learning about human rights in schools.

The impact of globalisation on the demographics of different nation-states has led to a renewed focus on civic education which promotes national loyalty and belonging, often targeting, either explicitly or implicitly, students from minority or migration backgrounds. Official policies for EDC may address diversity, yet they do so from a strongly national (and sometimes nationalist) perspective. In our global age we need a new type of citizenship education which challenges some commonly held assumptions about citizenship learning in schools. We begin by critiquing the commonly pursued model of education for national citizenship.

Citizenship education and the nation-state

At the beginning of the twenty-first century, citizenship education programmes typically remain focused on the nation and citizens' supposed natural affinity to the nation-state (Osler and Starkey, 2006; Reid, Gill and Sears, 2010). Through examining and critiquing the relationship between civic or citizenship education and the nation-state, in the context of globalisation, it is possible to conceive of an alternative approach, namely, education for cosmopolitan citizenship.

In order to examine education for citizenship, it is helpful to consider national citizenship as a status, a feeling and a practice (Osler and Starkey, 2005). This enables a study of how education for citizenship is constructed to support a primary affinity to the nation, considering some of the pitfalls and tensions which arise when such policies are pursued.

Citizenship is most commonly conceived by governmental bodies as a status. In this sense citizenship is synonymous with nationality. Citizenship as status is, in many ways, exclusive: although individuals can hold dual citizenship, so that, for example, an individual can be a Pakistani citizen and a British citizen (holding two passports); either a person is a citizen of a nation-state, or s/he is not. This conception of citizenship contrasts with the status of all individuals as holders of human rights. The status of human rights holder, unlike that of citizenship, is inclusive. All human beings, including those who are stateless, are holders of human rights.

Citizenship can also be conceived as a feeling or sense of belonging. The degree to which a person feels they belong is not necessarily related to formal status, although legal entitlements obtained through citizenship status may be among those goods which enable a person to feel they belong. Prerequisites for belonging are likely to include: access to services and resources; legal rights of residence; social and psychological security; an absence of discrimination and/or legal redress if discrimination occurs; and acceptance by others within the community.

Citizenship can also be conceptualised as practice. Citizenship as practice is the everyday citizenship engagement in which each individual can participate, in working alongside others to make a difference. Citizenship in this sense is the everyday political, social, economic and cultural activities in which people engage to shape the community, most commonly in the immediate locality or at the level of a town or city, but also at other scales, including national and global.

Citizenship as status, feeling and practice are interlinked: citizenship status may give an individual a sense of security and enable them to feel they belong and so enhance their engagement in the affairs of the community. Nevertheless, the three elements are also discrete; so, for example, it is not necessary to have citizenship status or nationality in order to be an active, contributing member of society, engaged in the practice of citizenship.

Education for democratic citizenship and national belonging

Education for national citizenship focuses on one or more elements of citizenship, but tends to emphasise citizenship as status. So citizenship education programmes typically address knowledge about the constitution and the legal entitlements and duties of citizenship, such as voting, knowing and obeying the law and paying taxes (even though these responsibilities are not necessarily restricted to those who hold the formal status of citizen). As in France, they sometimes target migrants and aspirant citizens, in order to induct them into the laws and social mores of the nation (Osler and Starkey, 2009).

This emphasis on knowledge-based learning is sometimes seen by policy-makers and educators to stand in tension with that of education for citizenship as practice, which is often locally or community focused, and is likely to include community engagement or service learning. Education for citizenship as practice is sometimes targeted at students who are perceived to be less academic in their interests, or who are judged to be lower achievers. For example, Scott and Cogan (2010) report that a course entitled 'Community Civics' was proposed in the United States during the second decade of the twentieth century. It aimed to prepare school-leavers to fulfil their roles in participatory citizenship. The proposal was in tension with what remains today a standard US knowledge-based civics education almost a century later.

The same tension between traditional civics and community-focused learning also continues in England at the beginning of the twenty-first century, where some teachers argue that lower-attaining students are better suited to locally based community learning than to knowledge-based citizenship courses focusing on the nation and beyond (Osler and Savvides, 2009). The UK government's Youth Citizenship Commission (YCC), which conducted a public consultation on a number of youth citizenship issues from 2008 to 2009, including whether the voting age should be reduced to 16, recommended that government should place less emphasis on the formal school curriculum, and instead 'encourage youth volunteering and also explore whether a compulsory programme of civic service for young people might be worthwhile' (YCC, 2009:49). It is envisaged that any compulsory civic service would strengthen youth citizenship and belonging by focusing this service on young people's local communities.

Nevertheless, education for national citizenship also stresses, in many contexts, citizenship as feeling as well as citizenship as status. Taking the case of Singapore, Baildon and Sim (2010) discuss the challenge faced by government of 'managing identities'. They report that, in Singapore, official discourse stresses a sense of belonging as something critical to the national curriculum, and to 'national survival'. According to this perspective, without such education, there is a real danger that young Singaporeans will pack their bags and take flight if they see better opportunities elsewhere. Therefore, they need to be encouraged to develop a stronger sense of national pride and learn 'the Singapore story', which recalls the struggles of political leaders and past generations. The aim is to encourage young citizens to recognise a duty and vital obligation to protect their country, and overcome its apparent vulnerability.

Senior politicians in Britain have also stressed the importance of a strong sense of national identity, through the study of British history and the British story of democracy, with such calls gaining momentum after the suicide bombings in London in 2005. In this development within citizenship education, a new emphasis is attached to the nation's ethnic diversity. This development needs critical analysis, stemming as it does from a concern about terrorism (Osler and Starkey, 2006), yet largely avoiding discussion of continuing barriers to democracy such as inequalities and racism (Osler, 2008).

Democracy, diversity and hidden histories

At the beginning of the twenty-first century, references to diversity within citizenship education policies usually imply ethnic and cultural diversity. Some policy documents celebrate the diverse populations of the nation-state, but fail to take into consideration the differential access that different groups encounter in accessing citizenship rights. They neglect to examine power relations or barriers to citizenship, historical or contemporary. As Bryan (2008 and 2010) reminds us, citizenship education policies and other related policies addressing, for example, intercultural or multicultural education, need to be contextualised within a broader legislative framework relating to citizenship, immigration and social cohesion.

History is sometimes harnessed to tell a national story of citizenship, as in the Singapore story, and this telling of the national story can be found not only in school texts and promoted through formal education, but also in museums, where it is often presented in a compelling way, as in the National Museum of Singapore, where it is retold for children and adults alike, and for citizens, residents and, indeed, visitors and tourists. In reality, in Singapore as elsewhere, there are many different histories to be told, and it is these different perspectives, when explored, that can engage young people as critical learners. In examining diversity, it is important to identify the silences around certain forms of diversity, particularly silences around gender and women's citizenship. In national stories it would appear that the citizen is rarely gendered; and that ethnic and cultural diversity is often portrayed either as new or as something which must be carefully managed. Political dissent is rarely seen as progressive, unless part of a struggle against a colonial power, or in a story where the nation has (re-)established democracy, after a period of dictatorship.

Interestingly, the British story of democracy is set largely within the territorial confines of the United Kingdom, and Prime Minister Gordon Brown has called for a new sense of patriotic pride, which aims to be inclusive and to avoid any basis in ethnic exclusivity and which will be realised through the teaching of British history. Unfortunately, the rhetoric ignores the multiple histories and perspectives of a diverse nation (Osler, 2009). It also ignores the legacy of empire. The modern international institution of the Commonwealth remains a key forum for international dialogue for many member-states, significantly within Africa, with key meetings reported in the media and regular celebrations and holidays. Yet this institution is largely overlooked in the British media, receives minimum recognition among the British public, and receives, at best, passing mention in British schools. Commonwealth Day is celebrated around the world by school children, but few in the United Kingdom join the celebrations.

Democracy and diversity

National political and educational programmes in progress at the beginning of the twenty-first century continue to draw a line between rightful, deserving citizens and an alien Other. Within this outsider grouping are some who hold citizenship status, but who are nevertheless portrayed as an alien threat. In such an atmosphere of fear, refugees and asylum seekers are no longer vulnerable people in need of assistance and with an entitlement to have their claims considered, but are portrayed as unscrupulous individuals exploiting both international law and those who rightfully belong. Reid and Gill (2010) show how the Australian government, under Prime Minister Howard, promoted such a message of fear, in the wake of the 2001 attacks on the United States, preventing migrants seeking refugee status from landing in Australia and making their claims.

In the revised national curriculum for citizenship in England (QCA and DCSF, 2007a) the British story of democracy is presented as a completed project, as it was in the curriculum's important founding document, the Crick Report (QCA, 1998a), rather than a process which needs continual renewal. Particular groups are identified as 'vulnerable', less likely to identify with the nation and therefore in need of specific targeted compensatory education. British government funds are thus being set aside for programmes aimed at preventing 'violent extremism' and the radicalisation of young Muslims (Home Office, 2008). The official title of this funding initiative is Preventing Violent Extremism, but there are concerns that targeting particular young people in this way will provoke antagonism, both within Muslim communities and towards them (Akram and Richardson, 2009; Osler, 2009). Effectively, whole groups of citizens are classed as having a deficit in terms of their loyalty to the polity.

Sears (2010) considers education for citizenship within the context of diversity, observing that the reconciliation of different positions has always been part of the Canadian framework. Following Kymlicka (2003a), he notes how Canada is distinctive in having to address three types of diversity (national minorities, immigrants and indigenous peoples). What is curious is that diversity in so many national contexts continues to be seen as a problem, or at best, a challenge, rather than an asset to democracy (Osler 2008; Parker 2002). The vision that democracy needs diversity (political, cultural and social) in order to flourish and regenerate is lost.

Education for cosmopolitan citizenship and human rights
In our global age, not all young people at school are citizens of the nation-state in which they are studying. Citizenship education cannot be premised on the notion that all students are citizens or aspirant citizens. A report produced by an international panel of scholars at the University of Washington (Banks *et al*, 2005) sought to identify some key principles for education programmes. It concluded: 'The teaching of human rights should underpin citizenship education courses and programs in multicultural nation-states'

(Banks *et al*, 2005). This principle should apply in all schools, regardless of the ethnic or cultural composition of the student population or the nation in question.

Recognition that all human beings are holders of human rights is also an underpinning principle of education for cosmopolitan citizenship. The human rights project is a cosmopolitan project, which assumes the equal entitlement to rights of all human beings. Education for cosmopolitan citizenship is a theoretical construct in which citizenship at all scales, from the local to the global, is reconceptualised. This enables young people to re-cognise our common humanity and express solidarity with others at all levels from the local to the global, accepting and valuing diversity at all these levels (Osler and Vincent 2002; Osler and Starkey 2003, 2005).

Education for cosmopolitan citizenship is thus conceptualised, not as an alternative to national citizenship education, nor, as has sometimes been interpreted, as a synonym for global citizenship education. It requires that we re-imagine the nation as cosmopolitan, and that we reconceptualise education for national citizenship so that it meets more adequately the needs of contemporary nation-states and the global community. It demands we acknowledge there are many ways of being Australian, Brazilian, British, Canadian, Japanese, Mexican, Singaporean, and so on.

Citizenship does not necessarily require a deep love of country; it requires minimally a commitment to the polity (Parekh, 2000). It is policy and legislative frameworks designed to promote greater social justice and remove barriers to full participative citizenship which will allow individuals to develop affective ties to the nation. Efforts by nation-states to promote national identity and affinity through education, in response to perceived threats, risk unintended outcomes, provoke concerns about propaganda and threaten, rather than secure, social cohesion and democratic participation.

Interestingly, within EU member states, an assumed binary between education for national and global citizenship (Marshall 2009) is troubled by the issue of European citizenship and belonging (Osler and Savvides 2009). Evidence is also emerging that many young people do not identify primarily or exclusively with the nation-state but have flexible and shifting identities (Mitchell and Parker 2008; Osler and Starkey 2003). At all levels, national, regional, global and especially at the local level, education for cosmopolitan citizenship responds to the realities of learning to live together and develop a dialogue with those whose perspectives are different from our own.

Citizen action, civil rights and human rights

> We can never get civil rights in America until our human rights are first restored. We will never be recognised as citizens until we are first recognised as humans. (Malcolm X,1964)

Malcolm X made this claim at the climax of the civil rights struggle in the United States. Although in 1954 the Supreme Court had ruled in the pivotal *Brown v Board of Education* that segregated schools were unconstitutional, racial segregation remained an everyday reality for American citizens in the Southern states. In July 1964, the Civil Rights Act was passed, which enforced the constitutional right to vote, and prohibited discrimination in public facilities, in government, and in employment. It became illegal, and therefore punishable, to continue to enforce segregation in schools, housing or in employment. The struggle for formal equality was not immediately realised, as it took some years before the powers to enforce all aspects of the new law were strengthened.

Malcolm X's statement reminds us that citizenship, and education for democratic citizenship, must be premised on recognition of our shared humanity. In those places in the United States where African-Americans experienced overt and structural discrimination, recognition of shared humanity required not only legal provisions, but also, over a longer period, a cultural and emotional shift; it required a recognition among individuals in white communities that civil rights meant more than a formal legal equality. This cultural and emotional shift demands the recognition that fellow citizens, regardless of ethnicity, gender, culture, sexuality, religious or political belief, or any other difference, are also human beings.

Our commonality is important. It extends beyond national boundaries and requires us to extend recognition of this shared heritage to those we live alongside who do not share our citizenship, and to strangers in distant places. Human rights are universal and all human beings, regardless of their behaviour or even their commitment to human rights, have an equal entitlement to these rights. Malcolm X acknowledged, towards the end of his life, the power of human rights discourse in creating global solidarities and thus strengthening the effectiveness of the civil rights movement in the US.

International and national commitments to human rights education

The *Vienna Declaration and Programme of Action* reminds us that education is at the heart of the human rights project:

States are duty-bound, as stipulated in the Universal Declaration of Human Rights and the International Covenant on Economic, Social and Cultural Rights and in other international human rights instruments, to ensure that *education is aimed at strengthening the respect of human rights and fundamental freedoms.* The World Conference on Human Rights emphasises the importance of incorporating the subject of human rights education programmes and calls upon States to do so. Education should promote understanding, tolerance, peace and friendly relations between the nations and all racial or religious groups and encourage the development of United Nations activities in pursuance of these objectives. Therefore, *education on human rights ... should be integrated in the education policies* at the national as well as international levels. (Vienna Declaration and Programme of Action, Section 1: Para 33, 1993, *our emphasis*)

The then United Nations Secretary-General, Boutros Boutros-Ghali, in a message to the World Conference, told delegates that not only had they strengthened and renewed the international community's commitment to the promotion and protection of human rights but had forged 'a new vision for global action for human rights into the next century'. At the centre of this new vision is the duty of governments 'to ensure that education is aimed at strengthening the respect of human rights and fundamental freedoms' and the expectation that HRE be integrated into national education policies.

Following a proposal at the World Conference, the United Nations Decade for Human Rights Education (1995-2004) was proclaimed. At the end of the Decade, despite some progress in the global development of HRE, it remained a long way from being at the heart of educational planning across the globe. Consequently, in 2004 the UN General Assembly proclaimed the World Programme for Human Rights Education (2005 – ongoing). The first phase of the World Programme (2005-2007) focused specifically on primary and secondary schools, with a specific Plan of Action to support this sector.

Challenges and progress in implementing HRE

A number of governments have made substantial commitments to HRE, although the task of implementing HRE into the school curriculum is one fraught with challenges. An examination of the situation in South Africa illustrates some of the difficulties that may be encountered in seeking to implement HRE policies, even when there is goodwill and relatively strong political commitment to the project. Post-apartheid South Africa is widely recognised as having one of the most progressive constitutions in the world, designed to support 'a society based on democratic values, social justice and fundamental human rights' (Constitution of South Africa, Preamble). The advancement of human rights and freedoms is one of the founding Provisions of the Republic of South Africa, as spelt out in the constitution, yet incorporating human rights education into the school curriculum has not been a straightforward or simple procedure. Rather than introduce a new curriculum subject labelled HRE or even civics, the education authorities sought to integrate HRE and awareness of social justice into established curriculum areas. The curriculum statement for grades 1-9 states:

> The curriculum can play a vital role increasing awareness of the relationship between human rights, a healthy environment, social justice and inclusivity. In some countries this is done through subjects such as civics. The Revised National Curriculum Statement has tried to ensure that all learning Area Statements reflect the principles and practices of social justice, respect for the environment and human rights as defined in the Constitution. In particular, the curriculum attempts to be sensitive to issues of poverty, inequality, race, gender, age, disability, and such challenges as HIV/AIDS. (quoted in Keet and Carrim, 2006)

Despite the central and symbolic place which HRE has been assigned in the South African curriculum, and goodwill among curriculum planners, the challenges of developing appropriate HRE curricula which allow learners to understand and explore the relationship between human rights and the specific social justice issues facing their particular communities and the nation as a whole have proved considerable.

Keet and Carrim (2006) argue that the absence of a coherent implementation strategy and consequent de-contextualised and ahistorical approaches to HRE have meant that learners in South African schools have not been able to access their entitlement. Efforts to infuse HRE into conventional subject disciplines have been further hindered by the complex processes of curricular reform which have been enacted in the post-apartheid era. Thus, an education in human rights, which is every young person's entitlement under the Convention on the Rights of the Child (CRC) and which addresses children's specific social and cultural needs, and is, in the words of the curriculum statement, 'sensitive to issues of poverty, inequality, race, gender, age, disability, and such challenges as HIV/AIDS' has not been made available to all learners as a right.

Notwithstanding the often complex challenges of introducing HRE, a number of governments have made significant steps forward in enabling learners to access their right to HRE. Sometimes these commitments have come about, at least in part, as the result of efforts by NGOs and committed individuals who have formed partnerships and lobbied for change. For example, in Taiwan in 1998 a group of political scientists and educators from Soochow University and Taipei Teachers' College organised a workshop to raise awareness of human rights education among teachers and teacher educators. They invited a number of international guests to speak. By 2004, following a change of government, HRE was incorporated into the formal school curriculum. In April of that year, the group of Taiwanese educators and activists group hosted a number of conferences of to publicise local and international initiatives in HRE (Osler, 2005b). Their intention was to gain the support of school principals and politicians in implementing HRE as a newly recognised subject in the Taiwanese school curriculum. Not only did they invite their international guests back to participate and share in their success, but they also arranged a meeting between these guests and the Minister of Education, to support a process of lobbying for more resources for the new curriculum subject.

EDC, shared values and the needs of minorities

Since the early 1990s, there has been a considerable growth in interest in education for democratic citizenship (EDC) from both nation-states and from a range of international organisations, including UNESCO, the Council of Europe, and the Organisation for Economic Cooperation and Development (OECD). A review of research literature and official policy documents has identified six key contextual factors which go some way to explaining this growth in interest, namely: concern about global injustice and inequality (linked, since 2001, to concerns about global security and terrorism); processes of globalisation and migration and their impact on local communities and schools; concerns about levels of civic and political engagement; a perceived youth deficit; the end of the cold war; and anti-democratic and racist movements (Osler and Starkey, 2006).

Following the work of the Council of Europe, there is a growing recognition of human rights as the underpinning principles of EDC at the level of the nation-state. Human rights principles tend to be explicit in the EDC programmes of newly democratised states, such as those of Latin America and of Eastern and Central Europe and in countries such as Spain and Portugal, which experienced a period of dictatorship during the latter half of the twentieth century.

However, not all countries make explicit the values base underpinning EDC. Britain, for example, does not acknowledge human rights as the values base for citizenship education within the National Curriculum for England.

Indeed, recent media debates have tended to focus on the need to emphasise British values and Britishness as part of the preparation for young people for living together in a society characterised by ethnic diversity.

In December 2006, the then Prime Minister, Tony Blair, identified British values as 'belief in democracy, the rule of law, tolerance, equal treatment for all'. Earlier the same year, Gordon Brown gave a widely reported speech on 'The future of Britishness' in which he listed shared British values as 'liberty, responsibility, fairness'. Citizens of other nations might well ask, as have many British citizens, what is peculiarly British about these values? They are in keeping with international human rights principles and might be the expressed values of any modern democracy.

The processes of introducing and implementing citizenship education into the National Curriculum for England provide us with an interesting case study of how EDC may neglect the specific needs and interest of minorities. Our analysis of the Crick Report on EDC in England, *Education for Citizenship and the teaching of democracy in Schools* (QCA, 1998a), suggests that the images and understandings of multiculturalism within this official document are problematic and that the ways in which it deals with questions of difference, equality and justice are inadequate. A key aim of any programme of citizenship must be to enable young people to understand the barriers to citizenship, including that of racism, and equip them with the skills to challenge and overcome such barriers.

Yet the Crick Report adopts terminology which reflects a lack of familiarity with the everyday realities of multicultural Britain. For example, it refers to the 'homelands of our minority communities' a phrase which is not only patronising in tone but which effectively serves to question and even undermine the Britishness of students of colour and their right to identify with Britain as their home country.

Interestingly, research which included interviews with members of the Crick committee revealed a desire among those involved to play down the political implications and assumptions of the report, with one member even denying the use of this phrase 'homelands of our ethnic minorities' (Pykett, 2007). Hybrid and multiple identities mean that many students at school in England, and not just those from visible minority communities, are able to identify with a number of places, including Britain, but also with other countries with which their families have a direct link (Osler and Starkey, 2003 and 2005).

Thus government support for EDC does not necessarily mean that the needs of minorities will be met or that students from all backgrounds will be provided with skills to challenge the inequalities and discrimination which hinder the full citizenship and participation of many from minority communities.

Human rights education implies not only the right to education, but rights *in* education and rights *through* education (Verhellen, 2000). All children, including children from minority communities, are equally entitled to a quality education which enables them to achieve their 'fullest potential'. The principle of non-discrimination implies that the nation-state has taken adequate steps to prevent school drop-out and to address problems such as truancy and exclusion from school. So, for example, evidence of differential exclusion rates between children from different ethnic groups (see for example, Osler and Hill, 1999; Osler and Vincent. 2003) and differentials in examination outcomes between these groups (Tikly *et al*, 2005) is a key human rights issue relating to the right to education.

School exclusion also undermines rights *through* education, that is to say, it threatens access to an education in human rights. Rights in education include the right of the student to participate and to be consulted in school processes and decision-making, which implies the introduction of democratic structures and basic legal provisions to guarantee learner participation (Osler and Vincent, 2002). It can be seen that the development of EDC within curricular frameworks provides an opportunity for the development of HRE or rights through education, but that such initiatives need to be matched by policy developments and legal safeguards which also protect children's entitlement to the right to education and rights *in* education. These safeguards are critical when considering the needs of children from minority groups, who in many contexts experience some difficulties in accessing these rights on the basis of equality.

Challenges facing human rights educators

The Council of Europe has not always distinguished between education for democratic citizenship and human rights education; the unspoken assumption is that they cover the same core ground and both are concerned about strengthening human rights and democracy. Yet, in practice, programmes of EDC and HRE may differ considerably in the ways in which they characterise the relationship between the individual and the nation-state. It is this issue which needs to be addressed if EDC is to be an effective vehicle for human rights education. We have shown how EDC may fail to address the needs of learners from minority groups on the basis of equality, and how it is not guaranteed that such programmes will necessarily prioritise the dismantling of barriers to full citizenship for minority citizens.

A further serious limitation of citizenship education programmes as a vehicle for HRE is that they do not generally encourage learners to be critical of government. National programmes of citizenship education may have, as one of their goals, the encouragement of allegiance to the nation-state and a sense of patriotism. Our research suggests that teachers in England may feel uncomfortable with such an approach, and may wish to avoid reference to national symbols, such as the national anthem or the flag. Nevertheless, regardless of national contexts, teachers need to remember that:

> Patriotism is a double edged sword ... The accusation of 'unpatriotic behavior' can intimidate teachers and students into self-censorship. They may bow to conformist pressure from powerful media, clergymen and the government as to what is legitimate and what is out of bounds.

> To guard against abuses of patriotism, teacher[s] should emphasise critical patriotism. This approach eschews the irrational 'My country, right or wrong!' Critical patriotism encourages reasoned loyalty; pride in the 'rights' of the nation alongside a commitment to correct its 'wrongs'. (Banks *et al*, 2005)

Our research suggests that in France, programmes of civic education are more likely to encourage this critical assessment of certain aspects of national policy. For example, civics courses address the right of workers to strike and to take action against policies of which they disapprove. By contrast, it is inconceivable that learners in England would be presented with an official programme of study in which the right to strike would be emphasised (Osler and Starkey, 2009).

One analysis of the citizenship education initiative in England has set out to consider the degree to which it is about making citizens governable and compliant, rather than encouraging a critical perspective in learners (Pykett, 2007). One key difference between HRE programmes and citizenship education is that effective human rights education necessarily requires learners to be made aware of the need to hold governments to account. Governments are responsible for securing our human rights. While we may only be able to claim our rights if others are prepared to defend them, we should not see human rights as an exclusive contract between individuals. Some HRE programmes in schools might be criticised for placing too much emphasis on the responsibilities individuals owe to each other (horizontal ties) and insufficient attention to the responsibilities which nation-states have towards their citizens and towards others living under their jurisdiction.

As we have seen, governments have an obligation to ensure that the promotion of human rights is a key educational goal, with the requirement that human rights education be integrated into national education policies. Across Europe, it would appear that the most common response among governments to ensuring that HRE is a part of the formal school curriculum is to integrate human rights into the citizenship curriculum. As Verhellen (2000) points out:

> Spending an occasional hour or two on the subject of children's rights in schools would clearly fall short of the obligation States Parties have taken upon themselves. Essentially, there has to be a shift in fundamental attitudes on respect for children's rights. Theoretical teaching on the values of human rights and democracy serves little purpose if these values are not also put into practice (2000:42).

If EDC is to be the vehicle for HRE then human rights, or children's rights, cannot simply be another topic within an overcrowded citizenship education programme. Human rights principles need to underpin both the content and the practice of citizenship teaching and learning. As the quote from Malcolm X reminds us, citizenship and education for democratic citizenship must be premised on recognition of our shared humanity.

10

Human rights, politics and schooling

Education can be part of a solution to injustice and violence in the world, but equally it can promote violence and injustice. Educators wishing to promote human rights in and through formal schooling thus encounter numerous tensions and contradictions. Schools are often places where the dignity of students, teachers and other staff is undermined as a result of disciplinary procedures, testing regimes, inadequate facilities or failure to value diversity and difference. In order to become human rights-friendly institutions, schools may have to embark on a process of transformation that is profoundly political. This process is likely to generate reaction, resistance and conflict.

The development of a rights-friendly school is a complex process in which all parties (leaders, teachers, administrators, support staff, students, parents and school governors) need to cooperate. A human rights approach does not avoid conflict; instead it recognises that diversity of opinions is a source of strength and creativity. Schools need to find pragmatic solutions that address these tensions and contradictions and which respect the dignity and rights of all parties.

The right *to* education needs to be complemented by rights *in* education and rights *through* education (Verhellen, 2000; Tomasevski, 2001b). Efforts to introduce a human rights curriculum without simultaneous changes to other aspects of school life are likely to be counter-productive and to promote cynicism and scepticism among learners.

This chapter considers some of the pressures brought to bear on schools through the widespread adoption of official policies that prioritise education as an instrument for supporting the knowledge economy. It reflects on the potential of schools to enable transformative education and examines some ideas of educators who have theorised this approach. It proposes a set of pedagogic principles that support education for human rights and seeks to demonstrate the implications of these principles for both curriculum and school culture. It concludes by suggesting that the development of a human rights respecting school cannot be achieved simply by reviewing the school curriculum. Ideally, any review needs to address both curriculum and school culture and ethos simultaneously.

Schools and testing

Governments in the global North have been greatly influenced by OECD educational performance league tables and have bought into 'a vision of education as an investment in human capital and an engine for enhancing international competitiveness' (Tomasevski, 2001b:22). This has led to a strong, sometimes exclusive, emphasis on school performance, driven by testing and inspection regimes. As the number of tests has grown, so have learners' levels of stress. Paradoxically, there is now a developing body of research to suggest that regular testing can undermine children's self-confidence and commitment to learning and lead to a range of unintended behaviours, such as self-exclusion and opting out of learning, as young people adopt strategies which avoid the risk of failure and/or the criticism of teachers, parents or peers (Osler and Vincent, 2003; Jackson, 2006).

In the USA, the differential and damaging effects of policies such as No Child Left Behind on particular groups of students have been widely documented (Meier and Wood, 2004; Shaker and Heilman, 2008). The UN's Committee on the Rights of the Child challenged the competitive testing regime in South Korea in 1996 (Tomasevski, 2001a) and the National Human Rights Commission of Korea voiced continuing concern about the impact of 'the perpetuation of entrance exam competition and academic elitism' on students (NHRCK, 2009:7). In human rights terms, exclusively instrumental approaches to education risk undermining the dignity of those labelled as failures. Additionally, the whole basis of testing is likely to be culturally determined and to favour candidates from dominant groups. As Tomasevski observes:

> In subjects where children learn the official curriculum at school, while a different version of the same events, phenomena or values might be learned at home, and yet a third one in the street or from television, testing produces results that differ from what is expected (2001b:23).

In these circumstances, tests often serve to ensure that students themselves feel responsible for their failure; a failure that is effectively predetermined and which has serious repercussions on future life chances. Despite the fact that this instrumental, competitive view of schooling is backed by very powerful discourses and supported by the biggest budget lines, it has been resisted by teacher unions, by school principals, by parents and by students themselves, who have challenged such a reductive vision of education. There are many examples of school communities struggling to promote an alternative vision of education as a site of creativity, dialogue, conviviality and democracy (Apple and Beane, 1999; Apple, 2008; Richardson, 2007). More human approaches to schooling are not only legitimate but also necessary if education is to be 'directed to the full development of the human personality' (UDHR, Article 26).

Transformative education

Human rights education is necessarily transformative since it is based on a commitment to social justice and cannot condone systems that simply reproduce social inequalities. Human rights education takes a critical approach to knowledge and to authority. Legitimate authority derives from a commitment to uphold human rights. When education systems and structures construct failure, they also affront human dignity. When schools fail to provide adequate opportunities to learn basic skills of literacy, numeracy and effective communication, they deny capabilities and therefore human rights. When teachers, parents and students demand adequate resources, campaign for gender equality, challenge racism, and address disability, they struggle against a system that reproduces injustice. For this they need a language to name the discriminations that they observe. This was recognised by Paolo Freire who highlighted the tensions between education for economic competitiveness and education as struggle for dignity. He asked:

> How can struggle be taken and in the name of what? To me, it should be undertaken in the name of ethics, obviously not the ethics of markets but rather the universal ethics of human beings. (quoted in Torres and Reyes, 2008:124)

It is not certain whether the 'universal ethics of human beings' is an oblique reference to the Universal Declaration of Human Rights. Whether or not this is the case, the 'ethics of markets' can be contrasted with the ethics of the UDHR.

Freire considered that educators have two essential tasks: denunciation and annunciation (Torres and Reyes, 2008). Denunciation is what Apple (2008:

257) calls bearing witness to negativity, so as 'to illuminate ways in which educational policy and practice are connected to relations of exploitation and
domination – and to struggles against such relations – in the larger society'.
Annunciation is working with a vision of utopia and exploring the possibilities of another world 'more just, democratic and humane in which people
come before profit and are never used as means to achieve other people's
ends' (Torres and Reyes, 2008:119).

From the 1970s, Freire developed a pedagogy based on dialogue, which he
saw as an existential necessity because it is 'in speaking their word that
people, by naming the world, transform it'. In so doing, they 'achieve significance as human beings' ([1970] 1996:69). His concept of pedagogy built on
the theories of John Dewey ([1916] 2002) who advocated schools as sites for
the development of democracy in a context of rapid migration. Dewey's constructivist pedagogical principles, also based on dialogue and learning from
each other, acknowledge the importance of respect for human dignity. Whilst
Freire rarely referred explicitly to human rights, his view of dialogue and his
concept of naming the world is one in which education is a means to achieving significance and dignity, which is an end totally in keeping with human
rights and human capability. Without dialogue and naming, humans are
deprived of capability (Sen, 1999).

Freire also theorised education as a liberating experience based on radical
democracy. He intended that all stakeholders (teachers, students, parents,
and community members) participate actively and on an equal footing in the
most important decisions that determine the quality and relevance of education. These include policy-making (setting overarching goals, principles, and
strategies); school governance; curricula and pedagogy; and evaluation processes (Torres and Reyes, 2008). Such participation is not inevitable, even
when it is facilitated. Commenting on an experiment in radical democracy at
the Citizen School in Porto Allegre in Brazil, Gandin and Apple (2002:273)
note that 'participation is a process that had to be constructed' (original emphasis). Training for democratic participation is an essential part of the
model.

James A. Banks, drawing inspiration from the US civil rights movement, also
theorises democratic schools and classrooms that challenge rather than
reproduce the inequalities and stratification in society. He envisages a pedagogy that promotes not only a deep understanding of values and moral principles, such as social justice, equality and human rights, but encourages citizens to take action. His concept of 'transformative citizenship education'

(2008:137) accepts that the actions that may develop as a result of educational processes based on cosmopolitan perspectives 'may violate existing conventions and laws'. He situates education as a site of struggle for a vision of justice and peace in the world. Engaging in transformative education inevitably involves taking risks. Struggles for justice may involve actions which are illegal, but nevertheless legitimate. Human rights legitimise struggles for justice. They offer 'a globally available repertoire of legitimate claim making' (Levy and Sznaider, 2006:657).

Martha Nussbaum (2006) draws lessons from schools in Bihar and West Bengal in India to present examples of transformative education. She describes how a literacy class for adult women included challenging the power of local landlords. The women celebrated education as a means of freedom from fear. In another example, a group of young women who worked in agriculture during the day, came to school in the early evening. The school adapted its timetable to accommodate them. They used drama and role-play to challenge the entrenched patriarchal practice of dowry, an example of education addressing real social issues through imagination and critical thinking. She contrasts these approaches with the predominant pedagogical mode of rote learning.

Nussbaum (1997) has identified three capacities to be developed in education for democratic citizenship. The first is the critical examination of prevailing traditions, habits and ways of life, being prepared to question beliefs and assertions. The second is learners' adoption of a cosmopolitan perspective and development of an ability to 'see themselves as not simply citizens of some local region or group, but also, and above all, as human beings bound to all other human beings by ties of recognition and concern' (Nussbaum, 2006:389). The third capacity is that of 'narrative imagination', namely 'the ability to think what it might be like to be in the shoes of a person different from oneself' (2006:390). Human rights education offers a conceptual framework within which these capacities can be developed. Human rights embody a cosmopolitan vision and provide a set of standards against which judgements about traditions and expectations can be made. Solidarity and reciprocity encourage narrative imagination.

Pedagogic principles for human rights education

In our previous study of human rights education (Osler and Starkey, 2005), we argue that the principle of democratic participation is essential to the protection of children's human rights in schools and that this requires schools to examine their structures, organisation and management. We have identified wide-ranging implications of the Convention on the Rights of the Child for classroom organisation, curriculum and pedagogy, school leadership and teacher education (Osler, 1994b; Osler and Starkey, 1996; 1998; 2000).

An individual's understanding of pedagogy is likely to be closely related to a range of personal and cultural beliefs about the way children learn; what is understood by intelligence; the subject matter; and the students in question. These beliefs, whether culturally-based and/or related to our own bio-graphies as teachers and learners, may or may not be challenged by the formal processes of teacher education. The rights enacted in the CRC suggest a number of principles, outlined below, which can be applied to the processes of teaching and learning.

*Dignity and security: freedom from fear (*CRC preamble and Articles 19, 23, 28.2, 29)

The student's right to dignity implies a relationship between teachers, other adults and students that avoids abuse of power. Teachers will be careful to avoid comments that undermine the confidence and dignity of their students, including the avoidance of sarcasm. Teachers recognise that the legitimate authority that they have to fulfil their professional role derives from a commitment to ensuring that the human rights of all members of the community are guaranteed. For example, it is the teacher's responsibility to ensure that those who are most vulnerable are protected from threats, including bullying, and have the opportunity to learn in an environment that is physically and psychologically secure.

Classrooms should be places where there is freedom from fear. A human rights perspective means that everyone in the community has the right to dignity and the teacher's own right to dignity should not be forgotten. Teachers need to establish, with their students, a classroom atmosphere in which name-calling and mockery are unacceptable. With respect to any sanctions that may be required, schools and teachers need to ensure that they are reasonable, proportionate and administered to acceptable standards of justice. This will require the participation of all parties in drawing up explicit statements defining the limits of acceptable behaviour and determining the nature of any sanctions. In any case, sanctions will respect the dignity of offenders and avoid humiliation, including meaningless tasks.

Participation (CRC Articles 12, 13, 14, 15, 31)

The principle of participation runs through the CRC. Constructivist theories situate learning as a social activity, where all can learn from others. This is in opposition to a 'banking' concept of education that sees learning as a one-way transmission from teacher to learner and where the 'scope of action allowed to the students extends only as far as receiving, filing and storing the deposits' (Freire, [1970] 1996:53). Teachers should be wary of extensive periods of copying information, rote learning and uncritical engagement with textbooks. In a human rights respecting school, considerable learning is based on debate and discussions; critical questioning; creative activities in-cluding art, drama and simulations; and student-led practical work such as projects and scientific experiments.

Students should be given opportunities to express opinions and exercise choice and responsibility in decisions which affect them regarding the life of the school community (Osler, 2010). Many UK schools involve students in the process of interviewing and appointing teachers and the principal. Students should also be represented on class and school councils. There are many models for these, but human rights principles suggest that councils and com-mittees within schools should involve representatives of all those likely to be affected by their decisions. Participation is likely to be recognised as authentic where processes are transparent and where decision-making leads to real consequences. Student decision-making bodies need access to bud-gets and have responsibility for the allocation of resources.

The capacity to make such decisions is not innate, and students need appro-priate training, information and support. Training and participation in decision-making and the exercise of democratic control can be powerful learning experiences. Schools should ensure that as many students as pos-sible receive opportunities to participate and benefit from training.

Identity and inclusivity (CRC preamble and Articles 2, 7, 8, 16, 23, 28, 29, 31)

The preservation and development of identity, including the recognition of the multiple identities that individuals may hold, is a key right within educa-tion, yet one that is perhaps the most easily violated. Teachers need to ensure that they meet certain basic requirements, such as correct use and pro-nunciation of the child's name. Respect for individual children, their cultures and families is critical. This requires teachers to value diversity in the class-room and to recognise that diversity and hybridity are essential charac-teristics of all human communities. It means seeing children's characteristics, whether cultural, emotional, or physical, as attributes to be built upon, rather than deficiencies. Education systems, schools, and classrooms that deny or marginalise diversity are likely to discriminate against those who do not match the presupposed norm. Children whose social and cultural backgrounds are different from those of their teachers, and those with learning difficulties or disabilities, are particularly disadvantaged in such systems.

Freedom (CRC Articles 12, 13, 14, 15)

Pedagogy needs to permit maximum freedom of expression of thought, conscience and belief. The responsible exercise of these rights and of freedom of association and peaceful assembly all require a range of skills, which should be developed in the classroom community. The organisation of learning needs to include opportunities for student-teacher and student-student dialogue. Freedoms are never absolute and so freedom of expression will have certain limitations, in order to protect the freedoms, security and dignity of others.

One way of conceptualising the limitations is to ensure everyone thinks about time, manner and place. The timing of an expression of opinion or contribution to dialogue must take into account whatever else is occurring in the dialogic space at that moment. Totally irrelevant or insincere contributions are rarely likely to be justified. Similarly, the manner of any intervention should be sensitive to the feelings of others and should in no case be intimidating. Like the time and the manner of contributions to dialogue, the place is also a highly significant context. The classroom provides opportunities to subject opinions and modes of expression to critical scrutiny.

Access to information (CRC Article 17)

The exercise of the right of freedom of expression is at least partially dependent on access to information and ideas, including information from the mass media and from a diversity of national and international sources. Teachers have a responsibility to ensure that not only does the child have reading and writing skills to gain access to information but is able to critically interpret visual images, in newspapers, video, internet sources and other media. Skills involved in the development of visual literacy include questioning, recognition of bias and discrimination, and those skills associated with the design and production of visual materials, for example, a photo sequence or video.

An appropriate pedagogy will permit students to identify issues about which they wish to learn more, analyse the mass media, encourage creativity, imagination, criticism and scepticism, and arrive at their own judgements. The selection and range of sources of information in the classroom is usually determined by teachers, within the confines of available resources. While the teacher is responsible for ensuring that the child is protected from materials injurious to his or her well-being, there is also an obligation to develop a pedagogy whereby children have access to information on a need-to-know basis and are encouraged to identify and express their needs.

Privacy (CRC Article 16)

The right to privacy, which is jealously guarded by so many adults, is often disregarded when considering children, in the context of the school, the staff-room and the classroom. Pedagogy should respect the child's right to privacy, with regard to family and home, and schools need safeguards, in the form of guidelines, to protect the child's reputation when sharing information about individuals. While recognising that we often ask personal questions of children in order to build upon their experiences, cultures and identities, teachers need to remember that there exists a power relationship between teacher and student which may sometimes cause children to reveal more than they might wish. The teacher should consider the context, and avoid situations where children may be asked to reveal personal information in public, as for example, in a whole class discussion. If the principle of the child's best interests is consistently applied as a primary consideration, this should not prevent teachers seeking information designed to protect a child judged to be vulnerable in some way.

These pedagogic principles have been developed for debate and for schools and groups of teachers to engage in a process of self-evaluation. We have developed a self-evaluation tool *How does your school environment promote children's rights?* (see Osler and Starkey, 2005, Appendix 4) which draws directly on the CRC. This tool for evaluating the degree to which the school is in keeping with the principles of the CRC can be used by both teachers and students.

Human rights and history education

History has a distinct role within human rights education. An understanding of history is important for all citizens in a democracy. An emphasis on struggles for freedoms at different times and in different places may help students understand the significance of human rights and help them to form their own opinions about the state of the world and their capacities for transformative action.

Article 26 of the UDHR requires teachers to promote peace, democracy and human rights, but the implementation of this overarching educational aim is a matter of professional judgement. There is often political pressure for teachers to adopt an uncritical or deterministic approach to national history. History should not be used for the instrumental purpose of teaching lessons based on a singular, prescribed national narrative such as an uncritical 'onward march towards democracy' (Osler, 2009:88b). In any case, such approaches may simply discredit history teaching as students, whose families have their own narratives, detect bias and propaganda. Indeed there is a danger that, if human rights and democracy are presented simply as the values of the current political regime, it may appear that the regime itself is being promoted, rather than human rights (De Baets, 2009).

History education plays an important role in informing understandings of the present, what may be termed the 'identification stance' (Barton and Levstik, 2004:45). However, 'this is very different from using history [teaching] for the explicit political purpose of shaping the present' (Osler, 2009:98) or for the interests of a particular political party. An essential element of history teaching is the development of skills of critical analysis, including the analysis of primary sources. These skills are essential tools in transformative education, as they are to the development of democracy and human rights. A study of history encourages recognition of complexity, and an understanding that there are competing truths and narratives. Ideally, it should build on the varied experiences, understandings, and cultural backgrounds of students.

Human rights education: developing policy and principles

Human rights provide a perspective that can inform and transform the curriculum and the school. Human rights education has an authority derived from supranational institutions. It has relevance in diverse societies because it promotes universal principles and standards. Although humanistic education can contribute to a culture favourable to human rights, it is only human rights education, that can enable learners to make links between their lives, the actions of the powerful and the struggles of others.

The rationale for human rights education is clearly articulated in the UDHR. The Declaration is intended to be, in the words of the Preamble, 'a common standard of achievement for all peoples and all nations'. It follows that the population of the world needs to be aware of this standard. Human rights principles provide a benchmark for 'every individual and every organ of society'. Individuals and organisations and institutions including schools are expected to keep the UDHR 'constantly in mind' in all their activities in order to create a culture of human rights. Human rights need to be internalised and then used to evaluate situations. The key mechanism, in the UDHR, is education, both formal and informal. Everyone has a role, since individuals and institutions are enjoined to 'strive by teaching and education to promote respect for these rights and freedoms'. Article 26.2 of the UDHR defines the right to education as inclusive of the right to human rights education. It states unequivocally that: 'Education shall be directed...to the strengthening of respect for human rights'. A similar formulation is found in article 29 of the CRC.

Whilst human rights education is clearly mandated in international human rights instruments and governments have an unambiguous responsibility to promote human rights education, the development of common understandings of what is meant by human rights education and how it is conceptualised in different contexts raises a number of issues that this book attempts to address. Since human rights provide a vision of the world as it could be, human rights education must expect to challenge injustice. It is inevitably transformative and as such is the site of political struggle.

Although human rights are normative standards and there is a core of knowledge inherent in any human rights education, a simple transmission model from knowledgeable teacher to supposedly ignorant students is clearly inappropriate. Teachers and students need to envisage education as a dialogue and to recognise that all participating in this dialogue have insights and life experiences that will inform their understanding of human rights. These understandings will be further constructed and enhanced through interactions with others.

An empirical study (Flowers, 2004) of the views of over 50 human rights education activists from governments, NGOs and universities, identified four key areas of agreement. First, human rights education should be explicitly grounded in human rights principles as expressed in international treaties. Secondly, methods must embody and reflect the principles of respect for individual and cultural diversity, while affirming universal principles. Thirdly, human rights education should address skills and attitudes as well as knowledge and involve the whole person. Finally, there is broad agreement that since the aim is social transformation across the world, human rights education involves action at individual, local and global levels.

Whilst these areas constitute the agreements, the study also notes how government actors, NGOs and academics each have different emphases, determined by their respective roles. Governments stress international cooperation and emphasise international treaties. They acknowledge the responsibility of governments to support human rights education, but as a means to promote peaceful coexistence within the nation as well as between nation-states. NGOs are more likely to emphasise human rights education as transformative and a tool for social change. They tend to focus on human rights violations and the importance of civil society in addressing them. Academics, on the other hand, are more likely to stress values, principles and moral choices, emphasising the human side of human rights. Although the three groups have their own particular perspectives, there is in fact overlap between human rights education actors. Ministries may well recruit academics, who may also be NGO members, as advisers or even as officials with a mission to develop human rights education.

Respondents to the survey were likely to be familiar with, and may in some cases have helped to draft, recommendations from international organisations that provide guidance on implementing human rights education. The earliest and still influential *Recommendation Concerning Education for International Understanding, Co-operation and Peace and Education relating to Human Rights and Fundamental Freedoms* (UNESCO, 1974) enjoins member states to support education that addresses global problems. There are several features of the Recommendation that remain relevant. First, human rights are defined in terms of international instruments. Secondly, there is a move away from dependence on textbooks to 'methods which appeal to the creative imagination of children and adolescents' (UNESCO, 1974:3). A third feature is that: 'student participation in the organisation of studies and of the educational establishment they are attending should itself be considered a factor' in the processes of education. The Recommendation stresses the importance of teacher education, the training of school inspectors, and the role of human rights education in the early years when attitudes and opinions are being formed.

The Council of Europe (1985) published a detailed Recommendation that further elaborated and defined human rights education. The emphasis, in Europe, is on developing and sustaining democratic societies in the face of intolerance, acts of violence and terrorism; the re-emergence of the public expression of racist and xenophobic attitudes; and the disillusionment of many young people in the face of the continuing poverty and inequality in the world. The guidance recognises that 'human rights inevitably involve the domain of politics'. In order to protect teachers it suggests that teaching about human rights should 'always have international agreements and covenants as a point of reference' (Council of Europe, 1985:2).

There is recognition that efforts by individual teachers will be undermined in schools where little respect is shown in practice to learners or teachers, an observation supported by research (Carter and Osler, 2000). Human rights education requires a whole-school approach and the creation of an appropriate climate where 'participation is encouraged, where views can be expressed openly and discussed, where there is freedom of expression for pupils and teachers, and where there is fairness and justice' (Council of Europe, 1985:3).

Following the 1993 World Conference on Human Rights, the United Nations approved a Decade for Human Rights Education that ran until 2004. It was followed by the World Programme on HRE (WPHRE) from 2005. The aim of the programme is 'education, training and information aiming at building a universal culture of human rights through the sharing of knowledge, imparting of skills and moulding of attitudes'. The pedagogical approach is expressed in very general terms, as might be expected of a global agreement, namely activities designed to 'convey fundamental human rights principles, such as equality and non-discrimination, while affirming their interdependence, indivisibility and universality' (OHCHR and UNESCO, 2006:1). At the time of writing, the Human Rights Council of the UN is working on the text of a formal Declaration on Human Rights Education and Training (United Nations Human Rights Council Advisory Committee, 2010).

Official statements and guidelines require interpretation in local contexts. This is a task for educators, in schools and universities working in partnership with civil society organisations. Across the world there exist projects that develop materials and pedagogical approaches for the realisation of human rights education. One development epitomised in Amnesty International's human rights friendly schools initiative, launched in 2009, attempts to develop schools as learning communities based on human rights principles.

The global movement for human rights education has the ambitious aim of contributing to justice and peace in the world. The achievement of peace and justice involves struggle, and teachers and students will encounter opposition and resistance. Educators who promote human rights start from the conviction that the work they are engaged in lies at the heart of education.

Epilogue

Human rights education is a contribution towards a broader human rights project of achieving greater justice and peace in the world. It is about enabling individuals to work together with others to challenge the ongoing injustices and inequalities which continue today and to identify with the struggles of strangers, whether these strangers live in distant places or in their own neighbourhoods and cities.

While human rights education draws directly on internationally agreed principles, set out in the Charter of the United Nations, the Universal Declaration of Human Rights (1948) (UDHR) and subsequent international human rights treaties, it also needs to resonate with the struggles of learners. This is one reason why we presented three narratives in chapter one. The narratives of others allow us to reflect on our own narratives, and may encourage learners to tell their own stories and to identify similarities and shared experiences with others in places distant in both time and space. Teachers need to draw directly on the experiences and stories of learners in order to enable socially and culturally sensitive processes of human rights learning and teaching, which nevertheless remain faithful to these shared principles.

Narratives also enable us to move outside our own immediate environment and to identify with the stories of people we might not meet in the course of our daily lives. They help us recognise that we may have much to learn from people living in our own communities or in our own nation, with whom we come into contact, but whose life experiences are sometimes undervalued. These include elders in the community; ordinary people with extraordinary stories. Such stories may encourage younger people to continue to struggle for justice, when the odds look set against them.

Of course, the narratives might also be used in a more direct way, to examine historical and contemporary struggles for human rights, and to bring lessons in history and social studies to life. The narratives can be used to highlight how there are many different histories to be told, rather than one powerful national narrative, as is the case in so many textbooks around the world.

Teachers might draw on the narratives to study international human rights treaties. They may invite students to identify which articles in the UDHR they can recognise in the narrative, whether this is through abuse and denial of rights or efforts to act to uphold these rights and demonstrate human solidarity.

One striking feature of the first two narratives is that even in wartime, when gross atrocities occur, human beings are capable of acts of human kindness and such acts may extend to the enemy. The narratives cause us to challenge the meanings of nationality and citizenship. They subvert commonly held assumptions and understandings about prior moral obligations to co-nationals, as boundaries between people are changed and re-configured, both for positive and negative ends.

As teachers and as researchers we have learned a great deal from young people in different countries around the world. From this we have learned to encourage young people to tell their stories and to re-tell these stories ourselves. In 2007, we were invited to South Korea to support an initiative by the National Commission for Human Rights and the Ministry of Education to introduce human rights education in schools. We participated in training sessions for teachers in the cities of Seoul, Busan and Gwangju, supported by the British Foreign and Commonwealth Office.

Gwangju is sometimes referred to as the shrine of Korean democracy, and it has a proud twentieth century history of struggle against oppression. In 1929, student-led demonstrations in the city led to a major nationwide uprising against Japanese colonial rule. And in May 1980, civil demonstrations took place in Gwangju against a newly installed military government, during which hundreds of civilians were brutally killed at the hands of the Korean military. Today a national cemetery honours the victims of the Gwangju democratisation movement. As we were driven to the conference venue in Gwangju, a Foreign Office official warned us that we might expect to find demonstrators against British engagement in the Iraq war.

A small group of young people were gathered outside the venue, with banners in both Korean and English. They were members of the Movement for Teenagers' Human Rights and they were protesting not against the British government but against conditions in Korean schools. Their banners read:

Korean teenagers are living in exam hell.
U must know the truth, that Korean education is teenagers-killing education.

The protest was not against human rights or human rights education, but against a school system in which they argued that learners' basic rights were not upheld and where examination pressures lead young people to suffer extreme stress and anxiety, leading sometimes to suicide, in the cause of educational standards and international competition. Interestingly, the young protesters were welcomed by the organisers into the conference hall where they took an active part in the discussions on human rights education.

Their engagement in the debate is a reminder of the central importance of involving young people in educational decision-making processes in line with Article 12 of the Convention on the Rights of the Child (CRC). Teachers and policy-makers need to work to ensure that there is a consistent approach both in educational policy and practice between teaching and learning *about* rights; democratic practices and education *in* human rights in schools; and between young people's experiences of schooling and education *for* human rights and democracy.

The final narrative in chapter one is the teacher's story, inspired by the prize-winning South African film, *Yesterday*. Students in Khayelitsha Township, Cape Town told us: 'You must see this film. It is about our lives.' They remind us that this narrative and other human rights narratives are about all our lives. In what remains an unequal world, our actions and inactions will have an impact not only on others' quality of life, but also on their ability to claim their rights. The challenge of human rights education is to challenge injustice and demonstrate a deeper sense of global solidarity, recognising that other people's narratives inevitably reflect our own.

References

Akram, J. and Richardson, R. (2009) Citizenship education for all or preventing violent extremism for some? Choices and challenges for schools. *Race Equality Teaching* 27 (3):49-55

American Humanist Association (1933) Humanist manifesto 1. *New Humanist* 6 (3)

Anderson, B. (1991) *Imagined Communities: Reflections on the Origin and Spread of Nationalism.* London: Verso

Annan, K. (2000) *'We the Peoples': The Role of the United Nations in the 21st Century.* New York: United Nations. Available online at http://www.un.org/millennium/sg/report/ch0.pdf (accessed 6 January 2010)

Annan, K. (2005) *In Larger Freedom: Towards Development, Security and Human Rights for All.* New York: United Nations. Available online at http://www.un.org/largerfreedom/contents.htm (accessed 19 December 2009)

Appiah, K. A. (2006) *Cosmopolitanism: Ethics in a World of Strangers.* London: Allen Lane

Apple, M. W. (2008) Can schooling contribute to a more just society? *Education, Citizenship and Social Justice* 3 (3):239-61

Apple, M. W. and Beane, J. A. (eds) (1999) *Democratic Schools: Lessons from the Chalk Face.* Buckingham: Open University Press

Archard, D. (1993) *Children, Rights and Childhood.* London: Routledge

Arnot, M. and Dillabough, J-A. (eds) (2000) *Challenging Democracy: International Perspectives on Gender, Education and Citizenship.* London: RoutledgeFalmer

Ashley, M. (2008) *Taking Liberties: The Struggle for Britain's Freedoms and Rights.* London: British Library

Au, W. (ed.) (2009) *Rethinking Multicultural Education: Teaching for Racial and Cultural Justice.* Milwaukee: Rethinking Schools

Baildon, M. and Sim, J. B-Y. (2010) The dilemmas of Singapore's national education in the global society, in A. Reid, J. Gill and A. Sears (eds) *Globalization, the Nation-State and the Citizen: Dilemmas and Directions for Civics and Citizenship Education*, pp.80-96. New York and London: Routledge

Banks, J. A. (2006) *Race, Culture and Education: The Selected Works of James A. Banks.* New York and Abingdon: Routledge

Banks, J. A. (2008) Diversity, Group Identity and Citizenship Education in a Global Age. *Educational Researcher* 37 (3):129-39

Banks, J. A., Banks, C. A. M., Cortés, C. E., Hahn, C., Merryfield, M., Moodley, K. A., Murphy-Shigematsu, S., Osler, A., Park, C. and Parker, W. C. (2005) *Democracy and Diversity: Principles and Concepts for Educating Citizens in a Global Age.* Seattle, WA: Center for Multicultural Education, University of Washington

Barton, K. and Levstik, L. (2004) *Teaching History for the Common Good*. Mahwah, NJ; London: Lawrence Erlbaum

Beck, U. (1998) *Democracy without Enemies*. Cambridge: Polity Press

Beck, U. (2000) *What is Globalization?* Cambridge: Polity Press

Bédarida, F. (1992) *Le Génocide et le Nazisme*. Paris: Presses Pocket

Berkeley, R. (2008) *Right to Divide? Faith Schools and Community Cohesion*. London: Runnymede Trust

Borgwardt, E. (2005) *A New Deal for the World: America's Vision for Human Rights*. Cambridge MA: Belknap

Bouchard, G. and Taylor, C. (2008) *Building the Future: A Time for Reconciliation. Report of the Consultation Commission on Accommodation Practices Related to Cultural Differences* (CCAPRCD). Montréal: Gouvernement du Québec

Bowring, B. (2008) Misunderstanding Macintyre on human rights, in K. Knight and P. Blackledge (eds) *Revolutionary Aristotelianism*, pp. 205-14. Stuttgart: Lucius and Lucius

British Library (n/d) *Voices of the Holocaust Information Cards: Anti-Jewish Decrees*. Available online at: http://www.bl.uk/learning/histcitizen/voices/info/decrees/decrees.html (accessed 22 September 2009)

Brown, M. (ed.) (2002a) *Human Rights in the Curriculum: French*. London: Amnesty International UK

Brown, M. (ed.) (2002b) *Human Rights in the Curriculum: Spanish*. London: Amnesty International UK

Brown, M. and Slater, S. (eds) (2002) *Human Rights in the Curriculum: History*. London: Amnesty International UK

Brownlie, I. (ed.) (1971) *Basic Documents on Human Rights*. Oxford: Oxford University Press

Bryan, A. (2008) The co-articulation of national identity and interculturalism in the Irish curriculum: Educating for democratic citizenship? *London Review of Education*, 6(1):47-58

Bryan, A. (2010) 'Common-sense citizenship', 'citizenship tourism' and citizenship education in an era of globalisation: the case of Ireland during the Celtic Tiger era, in A. Reid, J. Gill and A. Sears (eds) *Globalization, the Nation-State and the Citizen: Dilemmas and Directions for Civics and Citizenship Education*, pp.143-57. New York and London: Routledge

Bryan, A. and Vavrus, F. (2005) The promise and peril of education: the teaching of in/tolerance in an era of globalisation. *Globalisation, Societies and Education* 3 (2):183-202

Bunch, C. (2008) Foreword, in J. Mertus and N. Flowers (eds) *Local Action, Global Change: a Handbook on Women's Human Rights*. Boulder and London: Paradigm

Bunch, C. and Frost, S. (2000) Women's human rights: an introduction, in C. Kramarae and D. Spender (eds) *Routledge International Encyclopedia of Women: Global Women's Issues and Knowledge*. New York: Routledge. Available online at http://www.cwgl.rutgers.edu/globalcenter/whr.html (accessed 24 September 2009)

Burchell, G., Gordon, C. and Miller, P. (eds) (1991) *The Foucault Effect: Studies in Governmentality*. Chicago, IL: University of Chicago Press

Bush, K. and Saltarelli, D. (2000) *The Two Faces of Education in Ethnic Conflict*. Florence: UNICEF Innocenti Research Centre

Carter, C. and Osler, A. (2000) Human rights, identities and conflict management: a study of school culture as experienced through classroom relationships, *Cambridge Journal of Education* 30 (3): 335-56

Cassese, A. (1990) *Human Rights in a Changing World*. Cambridge: Polity Press

Castles, S. (2004) Migration, citizenship and education, in J. A. Banks (ed.) *Diversity and Citizenship Education: Global Perspectives*, pp.17-48. San Francisco: Jossey-Bass

Castles, S. (2009) World population movements, diversity and education, in J. A. Banks (ed.) *The Routledge International Companion to Multicultural Education*. New York: Routledge

Chaurasia, G. (2000) Foreword, in H. Talesra, N. Pancholy and M. L. Nagda (eds) *Human Rights Education: A Global Perspective*. New Delhi: Regency

Clark, A. M. (2001) *Diplomacy of Conscience: Amnesty International and Changing Human Rights Norms*. Princeton, NJ: Princeton University Press

Clark, S. (ed.) (1992) *Malcolm X February 1965: The Final Speeches*. New York: Pathfinder

Commission on Wartime Relocation and Internment of Civilians (CWRIC) ([1983] 1996) *Personal Justice Denied: Report of the Commission on Wartime Relocation and Internment of Civilians*. Seattle: University of Washington Press

Committee on the Rights of the Child (2008) *Concluding Observations of the Committee on the Rights of the Child: United Kingdom of Great Britain and Northern Ireland* CRC/C/GBR/CO/4. Geneva: Office of the High Commissioner for Human Rights (OHCHR)). Available online at: http://www2.ohchr.org/english/bodies/crc/docs/AdvanceVersions/CRC.C.GBR.CO.4.pdf (accessed 17 December 2009)

Corner, L. (2008) *Making the MDGs Work for All: Gender-Responsive Rights-Based Approaches to the MDGs*. New York: UN Development Fund for Women UNIFEM

Council of Europe (1985) *Recommendation no. R(85)7 of the Committee of Ministers to Member States on Teaching and Learning about Human Rights in Schools*. Strasbourg: Council of Europe. Available online at: https://wcd.coe.int/cominstranet.InstraServlet?command=com.instranet.Cmd BlobGet&InstranetImage=605110&SecMode=1&DocId=686454&Usage=2 (accessed 8 January 2010)

De Baets, A. (2009) The impact of the Universal Declaration of Human Rights on the study of history. *History and Theory*, 48 (1):20-43

Department for Education and Skills (DfES) (2007) *Diversity and Citizenship: Curriculum Review (Ajegbo Review)*. London: DfES

Dewey, J. ([1916] 2002) Democracy and education: an introduction to the philosophy of education, in S. J. Maxcy (ed.) *John Dewey and American Education* vol. 3. Bristol: Thoemmes

Donnelly, J. (2003) *Universal Human Rights in Theory and Practice* (2nd edition). Ithaca, NY and London: Cornell University Press

Donnelly, J. (2007) The relative universality of human rights. *Human Rights Quarterly* 29 (2):281-306

Douzinas, C. (2000) *The End of Human Rights: Critical Legal Thought at the Turn of the Century*. Oxford: Hart

Eddy, K. (2007) On revaluing the currency of human rights. *Politics, Philosophy and Economics* 6 (3):307-28

Essed, P. ([1984] 2002) Everyday racism: a new approach to the study of racism, in P. Essed and D. Goldberg (eds) *Race Critical Theories*. Oxford: Blackwell

Essed, P. and Goldberg, D. (eds) (2002) *Race Critical Theories*. Oxford: Blackwell

Fielding, M. (2004) 'New wave' student voice and the renewal of civic society. *London Review of Education* 2 (3):197-217

Figueroa, P. (2000) Citizenship education for a plural society, in A. Osler (ed.) *Citizenship and Democracy in Schools: Diversity, Identity, Equality*, pp.47-62. Stoke-on-Trent: Trentham

Flowers, N. (2004) How to define human rights education? A complex answer to a simple question, in V. Georgi and M. Seberich (eds) *International Perspectives in Human Rights Education* 112, pp.105-27. Gutersloh: Bertelsmann Foundation

Foreign and Commonwealth Office (2009) *Forced Marriage Unit*. Available online at http://www.fco.gov.uk/en/fco-in-action/nationals/forced-marriage-unit/ (accessed 25 September 2009)

Freeman, M. (1992) Introduction: rights, ideology and children, in M. Freeman and P. Veerman (eds) *The Ideologies of Children's Rights*. Dordrecht: Martinus Nijhoff

Freeman, M. (2002) *Human rights: an interdisciplinary approach*. Cambridge: Polity

Freire, P. ([1970] 1996) *Pedagogy of the Oppressed*. Harmondsworth: Penguin

Friedman, E. (1995) Women's human rights: the emergence of a movement, in J. Peters and A. Wolper (eds) *Women's Rights, Human Rights: International Feminist Perspectives*. London: Routledge

Gandin, L. and Apple, M. W. (2002) Challenging neo-liberalism, building democracy: creating the citizen school in Porto Alegre, Brazil. *Journal of Education Policy* 17 (2):259-79

Giddens, A. (1990) *The Consequences of Modernity*. Cambridge: Polity

Gilroy, P. (1987) *There Ain't No Black in the Union Jack*. London: Hutchinson

Glasius, M., Kaldor, M. and Anheier, H. (eds) (2006) *Global Civil Society 2005/6*. London: Sage

Glendon, M. (2001) *A World Made New: Eleanor Roosevelt and the Universal Declaration of Human Rights*. New York: Random House

Gray, J. (2007) *Black Mass: Apocalyptic Religion and the Death of Utopia*. London: Allen Lane

Grover, S. (2007) Children's right to be educated for tolerance: minority rights and inclusion. *Education and the Law* 19 (1):59-70

Grugel, J. and Piper, N. (2009) Do rights promote development? *Global Social Policy* 9 (1):79-98

Hall, S. (2000) Multicultural citizens, monocultural citizenship?, in N. Pearce and J. Hallgarten (eds) *Tomorrow's Citizens: Critical Debates in Citizenship and Education*. London: Institute for Public Policy Research

Halliday, F. (1995) *Islam and the Myth of Confrontation: Religion and Politics in the Middle East*. London: I B Tauris

Halpin, D. (2003) *Hope and Education: The Role of the Utopian Imagination*. London: Routledge Falmer

Harber, C. (2004) *Schooling as Violence: How Schools Harm Pupils and Societies*. London: RoutledgeFalmer

Hart, S. N. (1991) From property to person status: historical perspective on children's rights. *American Psychologist* 46 (1):53-9

Holden, C. and Clough, N. (eds) (1998) *Children as Citizens: Education for Participation in Democracies Old and New*. London: Jessica Kingsley

Home Office (2008) *£12.5m Allocated to Prevent Violent Extremism*. London: Office for Security and Counter-terrorism. Available at: http://security.homeoffi ce.gov.uk/news-publications/news-speeches/millions-fight-extremism (accessed 19 June 2009)

Hopgood, S. (2006) *Keepers of the Flame: Understanding Amnesty International*. London: Cornell University Press

Hunt, L. (2007) *Inventing Human Rights: A History*. London and New York: Norton

Huntington, S. (1996) *The Clash of Civilizations and the Remaking of World Order*. New York: Simon and Schuster

Ishay, M. (2004) *The History of Human Rights: From Ancient Times to the Globalization Era*. Berkeley CA: University of California Press

Jackson, C. (2006) *Lads and Ladettes in School: Gender and a Fear of Failure.* Maidenhead: Open University Press

Keet, A. and Carrim, N. (2006) Human rights education and curricular reform in South Africa. *Journal of Social Science Education,* 2006 (1). Available online at http://www.jsse.org/2006/2006-1/jsse-1-2006/keet-carrim-s-africa.htm (accessed 29 September 2009)

Kershaw, I. (1995) The extinction of human rights in Nazi Germany, in O. Hufton (ed.) *Historical Change and Human Rights: The Oxford Amnesty Lectures 1994.* New York: Basic Books

Klug, F. (2000) *Values for a Godless Age: the Story of the UK's new Bill of Rights.* Harmondsworth: Penguin

Koenig, M. and De Guchteneire, P. (eds) (2007) *Democracy and Human Rights in Multicultural Societies.* Aldershot: Ashgate

Kymlicka, W. (2003a) Being Canadian. *Government and Opposition* 38 (3):357-85

Kymlicka, W. (2003b) Multicultural states and intercultural citizens. *Theory and Research in Education* 1 (2):147-69

Landman, T. (2006) *Studying Human Rights.* Abingdon and New York: Routledge

Lansdown, G. (2007) *A Human Rights-Based Approach to Education for All.* New York and Paris: UNICEF and UNESCO.

Laqueur, W. and Rubin, B. (1979) *The Human Rights Reader.* New York: Meridian

Levy, D. and Sznaider, N. (2006) Sovereignty transformed: a sociology of human rights. *British Journal of Sociology* 57 (4):657-76

Lundy, L. (2007) 'Voice' is not enough: conceptualizing Article 12 of the United Nations Convention on the Rights of the Child. *British Educational Research Journal* 33 (6):927-42

Mak, G. (2008) Diversity in the Chinese classroom in changing contexts. *Evaluation and Research in Education* 21 (3):252-66

Malcolm X (1964) Racism: the Cancer that is Destroying America. *Egyptian Gazette* 25 August. Available online at http://www.africawithin.com/malcolmx/quotes.htm (accessed 21 December 2009)

Mandel, R. (2008) *Cosmopolitan Anxieties: Turkish Challenges to Citizenship and Belonging in Germany.* Durham, NC: Duke University Press

Mannheim, K. ([1936] 1991) *Ideology and Utopia: An Introduction to the Sociology of Knowledge.* London: Routledge

Manokha, I. (2009) Foucault's concept of power and the global discourse of human rights. *Global Society* 23 (4):429-52

Marshall, H. (2009) Educating the European citizen in the global age: engaging with the post-national and identifying a research agenda. *Journal of Curriculum Studies* 41 (2):247-67

Matsuura, K. (2002) Foreword, in *Unesco (ed.) Universal Declaration on Cultural Diversity.* Paris: Unesco. Available online at: http://unesdoc.unesco.org/images/0012/001271/127160m.pdf (accessed 15 December 2009)

Mayo, M. (2005) *Global Citizens: Social Movements and the Challenge of Globalization.* London: Zed Books

McLuhan, M. (1962) *The Gutenberg Galaxy: the Making of Typographic Man.* London: Routledge and Kegan Paul

Meier, D. and Wood, G. (eds) (2004) *Many Children Left Behind : How the No Child Left Behind Act is Damaging our Children and our Schools.* Boston: Beacon

Merry, S. E. (2006) *Human Rights and Gender Violence: Translating International Law into Local Justice.* Chicago: Chicago University Press

Mertus, J. and Flowers, N. (2008) *Local Action, Global Change: A Handbook on Women's Human Rights.* Boulder and London: Paradigm

Mitchell, K. and Parker, W.C. (2008) 'I pledge allegiance to ... '. Flexible citizenship and shifting scales of belonging. *Teachers College Record* 110 (4):775-804

Morsink, J. (1999) *The Universal Declaration of Human Rights: Origins, Drafting and Intent.* Philadelphia: University of Pennsylvania Press

Murray, H. (2008) Curriculum wars: national identity in education. *London Review of Education* 6 (1):39-46

Nash, K. (2009) *The Cultural Politics of Human Rights: Comparing the US and the UK.* Cambridge: Cambridge University Press

National Human Rights Commission of the Republic of Korea (NHRCRK) (2009) *Submission by National Human Rights Commission of the Republic of Korea to the Forty Third Session of the Committee on the Economic, Social and Cultural Rights in Connection with the Consideration of the Third Periodic Report of the Republic of Korea.* Seoul: NHRCRK

Nieto, S. and Bode, P. (2008) *Affirming Diversity: The Sociopolitical Context of Multicultural Education* (5th edition). London: Pearson

Nussbaum, M. (1997) *Cultivating Humanity: a Classical Defense of Reform in Liberal Education.* London: Harvard University Press

Nussbaum, M. (2006) Education and democratic citizenship: capabilities and quality education. *Journal of Human Development and Capabilities* 7 (3):385-95

Nyamu-Musembi, C. (2005) Towards an actor-oriented perspective on human rights, in N. Kabeer (ed.) *Inclusive Citizenship: Meanings and Expressions,* pp.31-49. London: Zed Books

Office of the High Commissioner for Human Rights (OHCHR) (2006) *Principles and Guidelines for a Human Rights Approach to Poverty Reduction Strategies.* Geneva: OHCHR. Available online at: http://www2.ohchr.org/english/issues/poverty/docs/poverty_strategies.doc (accessed 6 January 2010)

Office for the High Commissioner for Human Rights (OHCHR) (2009) *National Action Plans/ Strategies for Human Rights Education.* Geneva: OHCHR. Available online at http://www2.ohchr. org/english/issues/education/training/national-actions-plans.htm (accessed 15 December 2009)

Office of the High Commissioner for Human Rights (OHCHR) and UNESCO (2006) *Plan of Action World Programme of Human Rights Education First Phase.* New York and Geneva: OHCHR and UNESCO

Oppenheim, J. (2006) *Dear Miss Breed: True Stories of the Japanese American Incarceration during World War II and a Librarian who made a Difference.* New York NY: Scholastic

Osler, A. (ed.) (1994a) *Development Education: Global Perspectives in the Curriculum.* London: Cassell

Osler, A. (1994b) The UN Convention on the Rights of the Child: some implications for teacher education. *Educational Review* 46 (2):141-50

Osler, A. (ed.) (2000a) *Citizenship and Democracy in Schools: Diversity, Identity, Equality.* Stoke-on-Trent: Trentham

Osler, A. (2005a) Preface, in A. Osler (ed.) *Teachers, Human Rights and Diversity: Educating Citizens in Multicultural Societies.* Stoke-on-Trent: Trentham

Osler, A. (ed.) (2005b) *Teachers, Human Rights and Diversity: Educating Citizens in Multicultural Societies.* Stoke-on-Trent: Trentham

Osler, A. (2007) *Faith Schools and Community Cohesion.* London: Runnymede Trust

Osler, A. (2008) Citizenship education and the Ajegbo report: re-imagining a cosmopolitan nation. *London Review of Education,* 6 (1):9-23

Osler, A. (2009a) Patriotism, multiculturalism and belonging: political discourse and the teaching of history. *Educational Review* 61 (1):85-100

Osler, A. (2009b) Citizenship education, democracy and racial justice 10 years on. *Race Equality Teaching* 27 (3):21-7

Osler, A. (2010) *Students' Perceptions of Schooling.* Maidenhead: Open University Press

Osler, A. and Hill, J. (1999) Exclusion from school and racial equality: an examination of government proposals in the light of recent research evidence. *Cambridge Journal of Education* 29 (1):33-62

Osler, A., Rathenow, H. and Starkey, H. (eds.) (1996) *Teaching for Citizenship in Europe.* Stoke-on-Trent: Trentham

Osler, A. and Savvides, N. (2009) Teachers' perceptions of student needs and identities, in G. Weisseno and V. Eck (eds) *Educating European Citizens.* Munich: Waxmann

Osler, A. and Starkey, H. (1996) *Teacher Education and Human Rights.* London: Fulton

Osler, A. and Starkey, H. (1998) Children's rights and citizenship: some implications for the management of schools. *International Journal of Children's Rights*, 6 (4):1-20

Osler, A. and Starkey, H. (2000) Human rights, responsibilities and school self-evaluation, in A. Osler (ed.) *Citizenship and Democracy in Schools: Diversity, Identity, Equality*, pp.91-112. Stoke-on-Trent: Trentham

Osler, A. and Starkey, H. (2001) Citizenship education and national identities in France and England: Inclusive or exclusive? *Oxford Review of Education* 27 (2), 287-305

Osler, A. and Starkey, H. (2003) Learning for cosmopolitan citizenship: theoretical debates and young people's experiences. *Educational Review* 55 (3):243-54

Osler, A. and Starkey, H. (2005) *Changing Citizenship: Democracy and Inclusion in Education.* Maidenhead: Open University Press

Osler, A. and Starkey, H. (2006) Education for democratic citizenship: a review of research, policy and practice 1995-2005. *Research Papers in Education* 24 (4):433-66

Osler, A. and Starkey, H. (2009) Citizenship education in France and England: contrasting approaches to national identity and diversity, in J. A. Banks (ed.) *The Routledge International Companion to Multicultural Education.* New York: Routledge

Osler, A. and Vincent, K. (2002) *Citizenship and the Challenge of Global Education.* Stoke-on-Trent: Trentham

Osler, A. and Vincent, K. (2003) *Girls and Exclusion: Rethinking the Agenda.* London: Routledge Falmer

Parekh, B. (2000) *Rethinking Multiculturalism: Cultural Diversity and Political Theory.* London: Macmillan

Parker, W.C. (2002) *Teaching Democracy: Unity and Diversity in Public Life.* New York: Teachers College Press

Pogge, T. (2005) Human rights and human responsibilities, in A. Kuper (ed.) *Global Responsibilities: Who must Deliver on Human Rights?* pp.3-36. Abingdon: Routledge

Power, J. (2001) *Like Water on Stone: The Story of Amnesty International.* London: Allen Lane Penguin Press

Preis, A-B. (1996) Human rights as cultural practice: an anthropological critque. *Human Rights Quarterly* 18 (2):286-315

Pykett, J. (2007) Making citizens governable? The Crick report as governmental technology. *Journal of Education Policy* 22 (3):301-19

Qualifications and Curriculum Authority (QCA) (1998a) *Education for Citizenship and the Teaching of Democracy in Schools: Final report of the Advisory Group on Citizenship (the Crick report).* London: QCA

Qualifications and Curriculum Authority (QCA) (1998b) *Education for Citizenship and the Teaching of Democracy in Schools (part one: Advisory Group initial report).* London: QCA

Qualifications and Curriculum Authority (QCA) and Department for Children Schools and Families (DCSF) (2007a) *The National Curriculum.Citizenship: Programme of Study for Key Stage Three and Attainment Target.* London: QCA. Available at http://curriculum.qcda.gov.uk/uploads/QCA-07-3329-pCitizenship3_tcm8-396.pdf?return=/key-stages-3-and-4/subjects/citizenship/keystage3/index.aspx%3Freturn%3D/key-stages-3-and-4/subjects/index.aspx (accessed 21 December 2009)

Qualifications and Curriculum Authority (QCA) and Department for Children Schools and Families (DCSF) (2007b) *The National Curriculum: Statutory Requirements for Key Stages 3 and 4 from September 2008.* London: DCSF. Available online at http://orderline.qcda.gov.uk/bookstore.asp?Action=Book&ProductID=9781858389806 (accessed 6 January 2010)

Qualifications and Curriculum Authority (QCA) and Department for Education and Skills (DfES) (2001) *Citizenship: A Scheme of Work for Key Stage 3.* London: QCA

Qualifications and Curriculum Authority (QCA) and Department for Education and Skills (DfES) (2001) *Citizenship: A Scheme of Work for Key Stage 3 Teacher's Guide.* London: QCA

Rawls, J. (1999) *The Law of Peoples.* Cambridge, MA: Harvard University Press

Reid, A. and Gill, J. (2010) In whose interest? Australian schooling and the changing contexts of citizenship, in A. Reid, J. Gill and A. Sears (eds) *Globalization, the Nation-State and the Citizen: Dilemmas and Directions for Civics and Citizenship Education*, pp.19-34. New York and London: Routledge

Reid, A. Gill,J. and Sears, A. (eds) (2010) *Globalization, the Nation-State and the Citizen: Dilemmas and Directions for Civics and Citizenship Education.* New York and London: Routledge

Richardson, B. (ed.) (2007) *Tell it like it is: How our Schools Fail Black Children* [2nd edition], Stoke-on-Trent: Trentham

Rivière, F. (ed.) (2009) *UNESCO World Report. Investing in Cultural Diversity and Intercultural Dialogue.* Paris: UNESCO

Rudduck, J. and Flutter, J. (2004) *How to Improve your School: Giving Pupils a Voice.* London: Continuum

Runnymede Trust (2000) *The Future of Multi-Ethnic Britain. The Parekh Report.* London: Runnymede Trust

Runnymede Trust (2001) *Reporting on a Report. Runnymede Bulletin 326.* London: Runnymede Trust

Sargent, L. T. (2008) Ideology and Utopia: Karl Mannheim and Paul Ricoeur. *Journal of Political Ideologies* 13 (3):263-73

Scott, T.J. and Cogan, J. (2010) A paradigm shift in the political culture and in educating for citizenship? The case of the United States of America, in A. Reid, J. Gill and A. Sears (eds) *Globalization, the Nation-State and the Citizen: Dilemmas and Directions for Civics and Citizenship Education*, pp. 158-74. New York and London: Routledge

Se, T. and Karatsue, R. (2004) A conception of human rights based on Japanese culture: promoting cross-cultural debates. *Journal of Human Rights* 3(3):269-89

Sears, A. (2010) Possibilities and problems: citizenship education in a multinational state: the case of Canada, in A. Reid, J. Gill and A. Sears (eds) *Globalization, the Nation-State and the Citizen: Dilemmas and Directions for Civics and Citizenship Education*, pp.191-205. New York and London: Routledge

Sen, A. (1999) *Development as Freedom*. Oxford: Oxford University Press

Sen, A. (2009) *The Idea of Justice*. London: Allen Lane

Shaker, P. and Heilman, E. (2008) *Reclaiming Education for Democracy: Thinking Beyond No Child Left Behind*. London: Routledge

Sinclair, M. (2004) *Learning to Live Together: Building Skills, Values and Attitudes for the Twenty-First Century*. Geneva: UNESCO International Bureau of Education

Smith, A. and Vaux, T. (2003) *Education, Conflict and International Development*. London: Department for International Development

Southall Black Sisters (2009) *The forced marriage campaign*. Available online at http://www.southallblacksisters.org.uk/campaign_forcedmarriage.html (accessed 25 September 2009)

Stammers, N. (2005) The emergence of human rights in the north: towards historical re-evaluation, in N. Kabeer (ed.) *Inclusive Citizenship: Meanings and Expressions*, pp. 50-70. London: Zed Books

Starkey, H. (ed.) (1991) *The Challenge of Human Rights Education*. London: Cassell

Starkey, H. (2005) Language teaching for democratic citizenship, in A. Osler and H. Starkey (eds) *Citizenship and Language Learning: International Perspectives* pp.23-39. Stoke-on-Trent: Trentham

Stein, G. (1924) *If I told him: A completed portrait of Picasso*. Vanity Fair. Available online at: http://www.writing.upenn.edu/~afilreis/88v/ifitoldnew.html (accessed 15 November 2009)

Swann, M. (1985) *Education for All: The Report of the Committee of Inquiry into the Education of Children from Ethnic Minority Groups*. London: HMSO

Talbott, W. J. (2005) *Which Rights should be Universal?* New York: Oxford University Press

Tan T. W. (1994) Moral education in Singapore: a critical appraisal. *Journal of Moral Education* 23(1):61-73

Tikly, L., Osler, A. and Hill, J. (2005) The ethnic minority achievement grant: a critical analysis. *Journal of Education Policy* 20(3):283-312

Tomasevski, K. (2001a) *Human Rights in Education as a Prerequisite for Human Rights Education (Right to Education Primers 4)*. Lund, Sweden: Raoul Wallenburg Institute

Tomasevski, K. (2001b) *Human Rights Obligations: Making Education. Available, Accessible, Acceptable And Adaptable*. Lund, Sweden: Raoul Wallenburg Institute

Tomasevski, K. (2006) *State of the Right to Education Worldwide: Free or Fee Global Report 2006*. Copenhagen: Katarina Tomasevski

Tomlinson, S. (2008) *Race and Education: Policy and Politics in Britain*. Maidenhead: Open University Press.

Torney-Purta, J., Schwille, J. and Amadeo, J. (1999) *Civic Education across Countries: Twenty-four National Case Studies from the IEA Civic Education Project*. Amsterdam: Eburon/International Association for the Evaluation of Educational Achievement (IEA).

Torres, C. and Teodoro, A. (eds) (2007) *Critique and Utopia: New Developments in the Sociology of Education in the Twenty-First Century*. Plymouth: Rowman and Littlefield

Torres, M. and Reyes, L. (2008) Resurrecting Democracy in Public Education Through Freire's Pedagogy of Indignation and Hope, in M. Shaughnessy, E. Galligan and R. Hurtado de Vivas (eds) *Pioneers in Education: Essays in Honor of Paolo Freire*, pp.117-32. New York: Nova

Touraine, A. ([1997] 2000) *Can We Live Together? Equality and Difference*. Cambridge: Polity Press

Touraine, A. ([2005] 2007) *A New Paradigm for Understanding Today's World*. Cambridge: Polity Press

Tully, J. (2008) Two meanings of global citizenship: modern and diverse, in M. Peters, A. Britton and H. Blee (eds) *Global Citizenship Education: Philosophy, Theory and Pedagogy*. Rotterdam: Sense

Turner, B. S. (1993) Outline of a theory of human rights. *Sociology* 27 (3):489-512

UNESCO (1974) *Recommendation Concerning Education for International Understanding, Co-Operation and Peace and Education Relating to Human Rights and Fundamental Freedoms.* Paris: General Conference of UNESCO

UNESCO (2002) *Universal Declaration on Cultural Diversity.* Paris: UNESCO Available online at http://unesdoc.unesco.org/images/0012/001271/127160m.pdf (accessed 1 December 2009)

UNESCO (2009) *World Teachers' Day 2009: 'Build the Future: Invest in Teachers Now!'* Paris: UNESCO. Available online at http://www.unesco.org/en/teacher-education/advocacy/world-teachers-day/ (accessed 1 December 2009)

United Nations (1998) *Rome Statute of the International Criminal Court.* A/conf.183/9. Available online at http://untreaty.un.org/cod/icc/statute/romefra.htm (accessed 23 September 2009)

United Nations (UN) (2008) *The Millennium Development Goals Report 2008.* New York: UN

United Nations Development Programme (UNDP) (2008) *Human Development Report 2007/8: Fighting Climate Change: Human Solidarity in a Divided World.* New York: UNDP

United Nations Division for the Advancement of Women (UNDAW) (1995) *Fourth World Conference on Women Beijing: Platform for Action.* Available online at http://www.un.org/womenwatch/daw/beijing/platform/index.html (accessed 23 September 2009)

United Nations Division for the Advancement of Women (UNDAW) (2009) *The Convention on the Elimination of All Forms of Discrimination against Women: signatory states.* Available online at http://www.un.org/womenwatch/daw/cedaw/states.htm (accessed 23 September 2009)

United Nations General Assembly (1994) *Declaration on the Elimination of Violence against Women.* Resolution 48/104 of 20 December 1993. New York: United Nations. Available online at: http://www.unhchr.ch/huridocda/huridoca.nsf/(symbol)/a.res.48.104.en (accessed 16 December 2009)

United Nations High Commissioner for Refugees (UNHCR) (1994) *Human Rights: The New Consensus.* London: Regency Press

United Nations Human Rights Council Advisory Committee (2010) *Working Paper on the Draft Declaration on Human Rights Education and Training.* Geneva: United Nations. Available at: http://www2.ohchr.org/english/bodies/hrcouncil/advisorycommittee/session4/documentation.htm (accessed 3 February 2010)

United Nations International Conference on Population and Development (UNICPD) (1994) *Summary of the Programme of Action. Chapter 7: Reproductive Rights and Reproductive Health.* Available online at: http://www.un.org/ecosocdev/geninfo/populatin/icpd.htm#chapter7 (accessed 23 September 2009)

United Nations Organisation (1945) *Charter of the United Nations.* New York: UNO. Available online at: http://www.un.org/en/documents/charter/index.shtml (accessed 8 January 2010)

Unterhalter, E. (2008) Cosmopolitanism, global justice and gender equality in education. *Compare* 38(5):539-53

Van Den Anker, C. (2007) Globalising liberalism or multiculturalism? The Durban agenda and the role of local human rights education in the implementation of global norms. *Globalisation, Societies and Education* 5(3): 287-302

Verhellen, E. (2000) Children's rights and education, in A. Osler (ed.) *Citizenship and Democracy in Schools: Diversity, Identity, Equality*, pp. 33-43. Stoke-on-Trent: Trentham

Vijapur, A. (2008) The right to education under international human rights instruments: examining education of Dalits in India, in A. Vijapur (ed.) *Implementing Human Rights in the Third World: Essays on Human Rights, Dalits and Minorities*, pp.71-98. New Delhi: Manak

Vilela, M. and Corcoran, P. (2005) Building consensus on shared values, in P. Corcoran (ed.) *The Earth Charter in Action: Toward a Sustainable World*, pp.17-22. Amsterdam: Royal Tropical Institute (KIT)

Vizard, P. (2006) *Poverty and Human Rights: Sen's 'Capability Perspective' Explored*. Oxford: Oxford University Press

Weatherley, R. (2008) Defending the nation: the role of nationalism in Chinese thinking on human rights. *Democratization* 15(2):342-62

West, A. and Allen, R. (2008) *Diversity of School Provision: Faith Schools. Memorandum submitted to the House of Commons Select Committee on Children, Schools and Families*. London: HMSO Available online at: http://www.parliament.the-stationery-office.co.uk/pa/cm200708/cmselect/cmchilsch/memo/311/ucm202.htm (accessed 6 January 2010)

Winter, J. (2006) *Dreams of Peace and Freedom: Utopian Moments in the 20th Century*. New Haven and London: Yale University Press

World Commission on Environment and Development (1987) *Our Common Future*. Oxford: OUP

World Development Movement (2009) *Water Campaign*. Available online at: http://www.wdm.org.uk/water-campaign (accessed 17 December 2009)

World Health Organisation (WHO) and UNICEF (2006) *Meeting the MDG Drinking Water and Sanitation Target: The Urban and Rural Challenge of the Decade*. Geneva: WHO. Available online at: http://www.wssinfo.org/pdf/JMP_06.pdf (accessed 8 January 2010)

Wright, P. (2004) *Human Rights in the Curriculum: Mathematics*. London: Amnesty International UK

Youth Citizenship Commission (YCC) (2009) *Making the Connection: Building Youth Citizenship in the UK. Final Report of the Youth Citizenship Commission*, June. Available online at: http://www.ycc.uk.net/publications/YCC%20-%20Final%20Report%20-%20July%202009.pdf (accessed 18 December 2009)

Zhou Nan-Zhao (1994) Educational rights: Perspectives and practices in China, in D. Ray (ed.) *Education for Human Rights*. Paris: UNESCO

Index